Copyright © 2015 Marilyn Harding

Second Edition 2016

All rights reserved. No part of this book may be used or reproduced by any means, graphic, electronic, or mechanical, including photocopying, recording, taping or by any information storage retrieval system without the written permission of the author except in the case of brief quotations embodied in critical articles and reviews.

Marilyn Harding
mharding1111@gmail.com
Aegina Island, Greece 18010

Because of the dynamic nature of the Internet, any web addresses or links contained in this book may have changed since publication and may no longer be valid. The views expressed in this work are solely those of the author.

The author of this book does not dispense medical advice or prescribe the use of any technique as a form of treatment for physical, emotional, or medical problems without the advice of a physician, either directly or indirectly. The intent of the author is only to offer information of a general nature to help you in your quest for emotional and spiritual well-being. In the event you use any of the information in this book for yourself, which is your constitutional right, the author assumes no responsibility for your actions.

Silver Arrow Publishing

ISBN 978-0-9869277-7-5 (Book)

ISBN 978-0-9869277-8-2 (e-Book)

Silver Arrow revision date: 12/21/16

MARILYN HARDING

Exhilarated Life

Discovering Inner Happiness

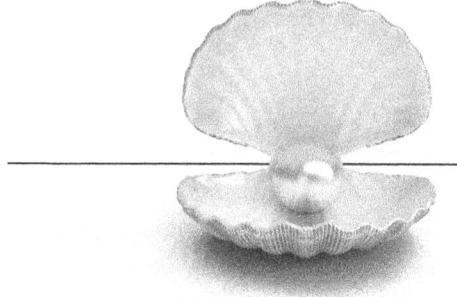

"There's a little something for everyone in *Exhilarated Life*. The product of a five-year journey through grief towards happiness, the book is at once intensely personal yet ultimately accessible. As we witness despair, bitterness, self-acceptance and forgiveness, juxtaposed with a deep love of travel, adventure and learning, Marilyn's humility and gentle, self-deprecating humor shine through her stories. Anyone attempting to cast off unwanted "stuff" would be well advised to spend some time in her company." **Bryony Sutherland, Biographer and Editor**

"Marilyn Harding tells all in this poignant memoir of a time of significant change and personal growth. The reader shares her failures and triumphs, whether they are financial or emotional, about life or about death. Marilyn's story is proof that it's the journey that matters, not the destination!" **Daryl Novak, Author,** *Biscuit: The Love Story of a Rescue Dog*

"*Exhilarated Life* is the author's truth, unabashedly shared with her readers. Without a shred of self-pity, Marilyn Harding delves into her past painful memories, and yet there is always a return to the bright sunlight of her resoluteness to embrace life again, through it all, with trust in the future. Harding's willingness to relate her personal stages of introspection on the way to finding her bliss shows a rare generosity. To read her delightful book is akin to basking in and soaking up an ever-youthful exuberance—and being so much wiser for the experience." **Pamela Jane Rogers, Author,** *GREEKSCAPES: Journeys with an Artist.*

"In an age where the "selfie" has become ubiquitous it is refreshing to come across a self-view that takes into account the emotional landscapes that underpin so many of our life experiences. What comes across are insights and some deeply considered views of how we have got to where we are in this trip through existence. The book is not a life map. It is, however, a guide to making one's life more conscious and complete."

"Having very much been brought up in the "stiff upper lip" tradition I identified with the author's reaction to the vagaries of life. Far too many of us are culturally ill prepared for the daily onslaughts of existence, and the writer's exploration of various philosophies, faiths and self-views become enlightening."

"I recommend this as meditations, where one can identify with the writer's thoughts and experiences, and rethink the message as it applies to the lives being lived around us." **Anthony J. Batten, Visual Artist**

"*Exhilarated Life* is the personal diary of the captain of a beautiful, strong and nimble ship caught in the powerful storms of Life. It takes us on an epic hyperbolic journey—the DNA-like relationship between our limited human psyche (the ship we steer) and unlimited Spirit (Nature in all its Power and Glory) with absolute honesty, weaving back unto itself the reflections and substance of a life courageously lived and deeply self-examined. I am ever humbled by those magical moments in our life, which help open our protective shell to fully reveal our most precious hidden pearls. *Exhilarated Life* is just that for the reader, the stuff of real "into-me-see," the potent and sobering brew of pure unadulterated Truth that wakes us up and sets us FREE." **Gita Masiques, Spiritual Teacher**

"An enlightening book covering complex spiritual concepts with everyday life examples that I believe will resonate with many people. Marilyn is a great writer—you flow along with her easy humor—she lightens up life's challenges." **Hilary Bowring, Author, *Find Your Soul: In Your Heart***

"Marilyn Harding is the scout who has gone before us culling the range of human emotion, psychology, and spirit, and reporting back, with bare bone honesty, courage, razor sharp intelligence and wit, inspiring insights to personal peace and freedom in a gem of a book she calls: *Exhilarated Life*." **Jerelyn Craden, Author, *Vessie Flamingo Outshining the Moon***

"*Exhilarated Life* is an anthem for visionaries; for those who refuse to be stuck in the circumstances of their lives and seek transcendence to happiness." **Michelle Murphy, Medium**

"*Exhilarated Life* is a book of truths and possibilities the *What ifs*. What if you're already perfect? What if you already have everything you need? What if you no longer have to strive and instead you can simply and gently thrive? Marilyn paints possibilities in careful yet revealing words, so that you can't help but believe that the What ifs are in fact true." **Lisa McKenzie, Business and Marketing Strategist and Author**

Acknowledgements

To my late husband, my darling George, who taught me what happiness actually looked and felt like, and who kept his promise to love me until I loved myself.

To our sons, Nick and Chris—two beacons of light and my constant source of joy, encouragement and delight, who show me how sublime it is to live your art.

To my sweet Athan, who continues to hold my hand through this grand adventure of life with love, playfulness and a fiery Greek nature that doesn't let me get away with anything except my authentic self.

To the cast of hundreds—family, strangers, friends and foe—teachers all, and without whom these stories would not have been written,

and

Any literary work, like Life, needs a conscious, skilled and discerning editor to ensure a happy and worthy outcome. For gentle guidance and the polish of this book, my heartfelt gratitude is to Bryony Sutherland.

An inner source of happiness
exists within you.

It's precious and, when nurtured,
engages your innate wisdom
to reveal your immanent purpose in life.

Your purpose is unique, beautiful
and necessary for this world to evolve
to its highest expression.

Contents

Foreword	xvii
Introduction	xix

The Creation of Pearls

It Is What It Is	3
It's What You Make of It	15

Gathering the Pearls

Athens

Opening the Shutters	27

Canada to Greece via Hollywood

Rose Petals	35
My Mother Didn't Cry—She Wept	41
Eating Artichokes Whole is Prickly	45
I Planted a Flower but Desired a Fruit	51
The Dragon Dies (1 of 3)	55
The Dragon's Teeth (2 of 3)	61
In the Eye of the Dragon (3 of 3)	65
The Wrong End of the Telescope	71

When do you Give Up on Yourself?	75
In Pursuit of Happiness (1 of 3)	83
Does God Have a Sense of Humor? (2 of 3)	89
Happiness—The Real Deal (3 of 3)	95
Eden and I	101
If You Never Lie	107
Awash in Lemonade	113
Let the Bells Ring Out—I Get It!	119
Finding Your Pole Star	125
The Free Range of Business	131
The Black Hole of Indecision	137
The Midas Touch	143
Surrendering to What Is	147
What If the Resurrection Never Happened?	153
Mother's Day	157
Pale Pink Cashmere Mind (1 of 3)	161
The Shame of Happiness (2 of 3)	167
The Myth of Happiness (3 of 3)	171
Santorini Sunset at Oia	175
After Santorini	179
The Meaning of Courage (1 of 3)	183
Sympathy vs. Empathy (2 of 3)	189
Lies Are Like Mice (3 of 3)	193
Love Like There is No Tomorrow (1 of 3)	199
Love the Earth Like a Mother (2 of 3)	205
Love Is All There Is (3 of 3)	211

The Shattering	217
I Looked Down and I Got Scared	223
Hollywood Hooray!	227
Morning in Athens	231

Aegina Island

Sailing on Cerulean Seas	237

Stringing the Pearls

Holding On to What's Precious	245

Télos

Staying Social	259
Going Forward	261
About the Author	263
Notes	265

Foreword

The most arduous journey is not from continent to continent but from the conscious to the subconscious, or the heart, if you prefer. The distance thus traversed is all contained in the small space of one's skull, but the painful, and always long, experience into what Joseph Conrad called the "Heart of Darkness," leads to Self-Knowledge. While for Conrad, the heart was dark (or "horror" as he famously proclaimed), for Marilyn Harding it has been nothing if not a burst of brilliant light.

As a healing mantra, "Know thyself," has had a long history, from Socrates through Shakespeare to anonymous gurus meditating in the remote Himalayan reaches. This simple phrase is a mystery and a puzzle only to those who won't enter the recesses of the heart. Marilyn Harding has wrestled with her demons to gain entry. What, then, is her contribution in *Exhilarated Life,* a wonderful blending of autobiography and memoir?

It is this: Whatever lesson, truth, awareness, call it what you will, she sets down in this highly engaging book, is derived from *personal experience*. When appropriate, she uses various and well-known ideas from the *Gita* to Carl Jung, but the essence she extracts from the fruits of her life is her very own. Herein we find close family members, friends, and the damage or healing they visit upon us. Perhaps most telling is her characterization of the "dragon," those little "pieces of misinformation in the psyche," that may come alive in a remark made by an overwhelmed parent, or a teacher making you uncomfortable in class. Whatever form they take, dragons wreak havoc. And this book slays dragons.

For those feeling anxiety over public events beyond their control—and who can deny how we agonize over man's inhumanity to man that fills the news every day with horrifying events in every corner of our world—the book has a wonderfully sane approach. For those moments when you find yourself helpless in the face of atrocities perpetrated around the globe (Gaza, Ukraine, the unleashing of racial or gender annihilation and mutilation), and feel that universal urge Hamlet expressed so well "to set the world right," I will point you to a brief excerpt from the book:

"There was a time when George said, 'If you have one flaw, it is that you want to change the world.' My response at the time was, 'Yes, and?' Now I know what he meant and I no longer want to change the world. I can't anyway. *All I can do is change myself and correct my own bearings until I am sailing with benevolent winds...*" [Italics added.]

The book is not a call for inaction. It is, instead, a call to start with one's Self first, before you can expect to effect a change in others.

There is much more in this book than one can possibly summarize in a Foreword. I especially like the succinct "Eleven Habits for Happiness," formulated in Part iii. The author is hopeful, and convinced, that they will lead to the promise in the book's subtitle of happiness, wisdom and purpose.

On a personal concluding note, let me say unequivocally that I have come across similar books before, and most of them were abandoned mid-reading. This one, however, caught me right from the start with its emotional sincerity and balanced approach. I recommend it to all who, like Odysseus, journey towards home and heart.

Professor Raman Singh, Ph.D. (Ret'd.)
Author: *Opa!* (Screenplay), *The Gazelle* (novel), short stories. 2014

Introduction

I really didn't know where I was going until I got here. Oh, I had vague dreams and desires, but most of them were an absence of something rather than the presence of something: The absence of fear and anxiety rather than the embodiment of calm and joy. I grappled with demons and surmounted challenges. I set goals and attained some of them, and failed to reach others.

Looking for deeper meaning and personal purpose, I began to scale the spiritual mountain to plant my own flag of bliss, hoping to stay there above my worries and sorrows and take in the unimpeded view of a beautiful world. But that didn't happen. Or, at least, not the way I expected.

But what did happen is infinitely more wonderful and sustaining than exiting the world as it is and joining the few on a cool mountain summit. I got more deeply *into* Life. Into my own human being-ness—all of it. And now my view is panoramic—literally, from a hillside overlooking the Aegean Sea. I am still full of wonder that I got here. Not to this island in Greece, but to the kind of life that is ever unfolding in wondrous ways. Whether it is to find the best unadulterated organic honey right here in our own village or to sign-up for an online course at Princeton University, start a new business, or write my books, the "I" of my fullest being is central to every adventure.

If I didn't actively interact with individuals of all ages both personally and in business, I might be tempted to think that I am here because I am at a certain phase in life. But I know that is not true. It is not about phases of maturity but phases of personal development. The desire for self-actualization that frees the soul to continually create; to know clearly that your purpose in life is to be exactly who you are, and to vibrantly interact with Life in all its dynamic is the sustaining force of personal evolution.

My sons know it and are living it in their early twenties finding their true selves through music. My professional mentors know it and are bringing new values to global businesses in their thirties and forties. My colleagues know it and are at various stages of burgeoning and ebbing careers in their fifties, sixties and seventies. My friends know it and live creating every day anew enjoying a simple life, rich in friendship, creative challenges and a sense of fun. I am happy to say that my friends include every age. In this heightened state of awareness, we naturally gravitate to those with like values. Thanks to the Internet, our communities are global and based on more authentic relationships. Happiness is ageless.

But there are so many people who do not get it. So many who live unsatisfied lives, or lives of quiet desperation. Many who deeply wish change and greater meaning in their lives but don't know how to begin. From the outside they may appear accomplished, but within, the soul is pinched or withering. How do I know this? I was one of them. It isn't by choice that we merely cope. Sometimes we don't know there is a choice. And more often than not, in the worldwide din of bigger better best, we can't sort the lies from the truths so don't even begin. What guru, what sign, what manifesto, what bestseller, what practice is the answer? The answer is none of these. The answer is in your own heart.

Discovering this is the key to the freedom, clarity and vitality that results in an exhilarated life. I was a seeker for decades until the dawning realization, as I looked out over the Aegean Sea from our little hillside house, that I had become a finder. And in the words of Abraham Maslow, I had shifted from *becoming* to *being*. I discovered that the bliss I sought was not on a mountaintop but deep within my own heart.

The troubles we carry are just that—the troubles we carry. When we choose to just put them down, we gain the freedom to face with courage and energy all that unfolds on our path through life. The way is simple but it is not easy. Much has to be broken and discarded—but only that which is not you or that which is limiting your happiness.

And like the oak in the acorn, our fullest reaching potential is within us silently awaiting the cracking open, the sun and rain and soil to flourish. Our highest Self will flourish if we let it. And when we let it, we are truly happy and our life exhilarated.

***

Note for the revised edition:

There is no time or space in the evolution of the soul. Like the sea that can be rough and stormy or placid, life beneath the surface is rich and abundant with activity and life. This is the domain of the soul. It speaks to you in feelings that ebb and flow. It follows the contours of your body and mind and absorbs all your living experience. It knows all that you are—the essence of all you have within to become—and it knows all that is clutched within you that you are not. These are remnants of an experience you once had that left a pebble of belief that disturbs your inner happiness, overrides your innate wisdom, and dams the flow to your life purpose: To be exactly who you are, fully expressed. I have continued to evolve, as we are all vibrant works in process. Life continues to be richer and freer as I shed obstructive patterns. Challenges—inevitable in this world—arise but solutions become more objective and enduring and welcome guidance toward my ultimate goal of fully realized self.

For this reason, I ask you to read these brief stories not as mine, but as yours. While some have dates, they are not time sensitive. Life offered me ways of unpacking the spiritual truths of both modern and ancient wisdom. They are timeless metaphors and will speak to you at a deeper level. If one or many have a message for you, I ask you to just stay with the feelings that arise and let the wisdom within you surface. It will.

If it's an uncomfortable feeling, just acknowledge it as such. It is not you, but one of those pebbles of belief that has lodged in your soul. It needs only attention—not analysis or judgment—to dissolve. Culturally, we are trained to identify with the negatives in our life. We attach to the pebbles and forget the far-reaching potential of our creative self. We try to unravel "negative" experiences, further identifying with what we are not. Read these stories with the trust in all you may be.

The soul has its own language and its own pace. Allow that. Like the sea that reaches every shore, our souls meet and merge when we seek the deepest unity of life itself. I am here with you as you read my words; the words that I hope will set you free to discover your inner happiness, innate wisdom, and immanent life purpose.

Me agape—with love,
Marilyn
Aegina Island, February 2017

The Creation of Pearls

It Is What It Is

In the film *As Good as it Gets*, Jack Nicholson's character, Melvin Udall, responds to the comment that everyone has terrible stories to get over. "Some of us have great stories, pretty stories that take place at lakes, with boats, and friends, and noodle salad," he says. "Just no one in this car." I certainly didn't have pretty stories growing up notwithstanding the lake and boats, and if you are holding this book, then I guess neither did you.

We all have stories that shape us and inevitably they are the unhappy ones. This may be because they have more intense emotional charge or maybe because they weren't handled properly by the adults in our lives. I know looking back, that everyone does the best they can with the awareness they have and in the circumstances in which they find themselves. If our perspective is distorted when we make choices, the consequences and the rippling effects will also be distorted and echo down the generations. What I can look at objectively as an adult, intellectually, is not the same as the reverb that unconsciously filters my experience and perspective if I let it.

The roots of many of our distortions lie within our families. We play out the scenes over and over, well beyond the family unit and into our social and work life, until at last we recognize the theme and are able to make clear, conscious, self-affirming choices. That is what this book is about. My resolve to change, and in changing, alter my experience of recurring themes, and from here to set my family and myself, and others who desire it, on a course of true and unshakeable self-esteem, confidence and complete well-being.

You cannot change history but you can change how history influences you: *The past only affects you if you think it doesn't.* I didn't want to share my story. For one reason, I have already picked those bones clean. At least that is what I thought until I began to write this chapter. The other reason being it goes against all my conditioning to "rise above it and get on with life." It seemed like whining and self-indulgence. After all, we all have sad tales. We incorporate them into our story and make the best of things; lead "normal" lives. But it is this very familiar theme of *rising above it* that continues to separate personal truth and self-acceptance from an idealized, unattainable perfection. Herein lurks the silent saboteur of happiness. The harder it was for me to sit down and write what I have recorded within these pages, the more I realized that I had no other choice.

My first memory as a child of two-and-a-half was my mother going "away." It must have been a Sunday evening because for decades later, those weekend twilight hours would be resonant with doom. That night my dad took my mother to the psychiatric hospital where she stayed for some time, undergoing insulin and electric shock therapy to relieve her depression. My mom would be "away" for five years. She wasn't in hospital all that time, but also stayed at a recuperation center in another city and worked as a nurse until she was "ready to come home." We went to visit her on occasion and sometimes she would be allowed to return for a weekend, but when the time was up, the parting was renewed sorrow.

My mother was diagnosed as manic-depressive and treated accordingly. I wouldn't know until I was much older that her father had committed suicide. She was fourteen when he called out to her, and she found him in the bathroom with his wrists cut and bleeding. He died, leaving his wife and three other younger children, my mother's sister and two brothers, one just a baby. I asked my mother once if she had truly grieved her father's death; her response to questions was always so emotionally intense, I wondered. That is when I began to suspect that we often label and medicate a perfectly normal response to a dreadful and traumatic experience. The family was Fundamentalist Baptist and I can only surmise the lid that was put on such an event, leaving it up to an external GOD to fix the emotional wreckage.

My father, whose three older siblings all enjoyed university and college educations, was left to fend for himself after a wheat blight in the west wiped out the family fortune. At a young age, with little by way of formal qualifications, he began a sales career. When my mother became ill, he took to the road and travelled, and was always away one or two weeks at a time. I dreaded those days and would lie in bed at night, fearful he would be killed. I would later wonder if this was his way of coping with a home life that was too emotionally demanding. At that time we had a housekeeper who came with her son, between my second brother (five years older) and me in age.

I absolutely adored my older brother, ten years my senior, and would watch him comb his hair into a waterfall curl in the front and a "ducktail" in the back. He called me "Pigeon" and taught me how to dance the Twist. He would roll his pack of smokes in his fitted white T-shirt sleeve and head out for adventure. Then, at fifteen, he was considered too much to handle at home and was sent to live with an aunt and various other families until he went to university. I missed him terribly. I can only imagine what this banishment did to his self-esteem.

Evidently my mother was resisting treatment at the recuperation center and the director advised my father to tell her he wanted a divorce, so her emotional support network would be removed and she would be forced to rely on her treatment alone to recover. I guess that did the trick because it set her determination to return home. In the meantime our housekeeper, as I was later told, was hoping to stay, and planted seeds of doubt as to my mother's capability to manage her family. But my mother won out, and that summer she returned home. As it happened, the housekeeper died of breast cancer that same summer. Her son, who was like a brother to me by then, was collected by his uncle one day and went to live in another quite distant city. I only saw him once after that. Nothing was ever discussed. Mother was back. The housekeeper was gone. My suggestion that we all live together was coldly ignored.

In these few sentences I am speaking dispassionately of events that rode on massive emotional turmoil. I have no doubt that the adults involved were treading a minefield without a map. I also know that their words and actions spoke one thing, and the energies were entirely discordant. There was always a strong religious influence on my mother's side, particularly, and on my father's the determination to do the "right" thing, based on his private Masonic-based convictions.

I was alone a lot, especially during summers at the family cottage north of Toronto. My mother had seen the tiny log cabin perched on a hill of red granite and fallen in love with it. It would become her refuge. Nature and the trees and rocks and lake would soothe me too. My relationship with God was a very personal and accessible one, like an "imaginary friend." But the GOD worshiped by my family was another matter altogether. My mother's brothers had joined a group in their teens called Moral Re-Armament, MRA, which was in retrospect a cult. They were volunteers and travelled the world for "The Team," making films about peace and racial equality. The creed was "absolute purity, absolute honesty, absolute unselfishness and absolute love."

My mother and aunt were greatly influenced by MRA. The recovery program which helped my mother re-enter family life and maintain her tenuous emotional balance was actually the basis of The Twelve Step Program later used by AA. It would be hard to argue with those values. It was a strong, cohesive entity tightly bound together by absolutes, and overseen by a strict GOD with a world-changing ideal. It would be a logical refuge for siblings traumatized by their father's suicide. GOD was in charge of everything if you just "towed the line." However, projecting the leaders' own distorted view and magnifying it through the voice of GOD was the edict that sex was for procreation—period. And any married couples that participated in the act for pleasure were considered to be destroying the family bond if there were children, and simply aberrant otherwise.

This point is rather important because it would explain why my mother (who became pregnant with me at the late age of forty) would drop into depression. Was she happy before that? I don't know, but she wrestled with depression forever after. Shame is a terrible, *terrible* thing but an extremely powerful, controlling device that continues to resonate. I once read a scrawled entry in a pocket diary of the year I was born. In my mother's familiar handwriting were words of such despair my heart broke for her. This moral imperative might also explain my aunt's suicide some years later, six months after her youngest child was born, also the result of a pregnancy in her late forties.

My aunt's suicide occurred the year following my mother's return and our move to the house down the street from my aunt's family. The memory of that Sunday morning is indelible on my mind; being wakened to my older cousin bounding up the steps, shouting to my parents to come quickly. I was nine. My adored cousin, three years older, and I then stayed behind closed doors in my room reading *Anne of Green Gables*, while I can't even imagine what was happening up the street.

Ironically, it wasn't until I was in high school that I "heard" that my aunt had committed suicide. I went home and asked my dad if it was true. He said it was, but it didn't really matter how she died—did it? Looking back now, I wonder at the tightness of the cap that was ratcheted down on that little fact. How could I *forget* that morning and the actual, terrible words I heard? My brother, two cousins and I were sent off to family we didn't know somewhere snowy for a week until some equilibrium was achieved.

I think it mattered very much how my aunt died. The energy and seismic waves of emotion are consistent with suicide and tragedy. From the time my sons were little I told them about the suicides. I did not want any fascination or allure to this way of solving problems. When my oldest son was five, he would comfort me as I cried for my beloved older brother who, in his late forties, killed himself as well. Not all family members agree with my transparent approach, but children's radar picks up all the subtleties of communication. In fact, our whole bodies are receivers and we get information on levels way above and below any conscious filter.

The morning after my brother died, I called my mom. Her first words were, "You know, I just saw a picture in the paper of a house that looked like yours." "Oh, Mom…" was all I could say at this deflection, and then she sighed, "At least I don't have to worry about him any more." At the funeral, I was devastated to hear the minister speak solely of my mother and her two sons. It was as if I did not exist. The revelation was that my mother's depression and subsequent shock treatment had seared out any memory of me as a child. In a time of trauma she defaulted to a place before I was born. It also shone a light on the fact that while we had a "good" relationship, there was a detachment that I know I felt but could never pinpoint.

The reality was that my mother was "well" when she had two sons and "unwell" with the birth of me, her daughter. My mother would often say, "I love you in spite of yourself." I never knew exactly what she meant by that, but I know how I felt when she said it. When I was pregnant, each time I was determined that it could only be a boy. In my experience, the worst thing that could happen would be to have a daughter. And in writing this book I finally recognized the source of that belief, and my abiding lack of self-esteem.

When my first son was born, a family friend, Martha G. Welch, M.D., who was conducting research at Columbia University for a book on mother/child bonding called *Holding Time*, contacted me. She was concerned with my ability to bond with my child, as she was familiar with the circumstances of my birth and formative years. I engaged with my son, eight months old, in her therapy and found it amazingly effective.[1] She was keen to have my mother and me do it, but I could not face it. I just couldn't bear the thought of looking deeply into my mother's eyes. I was afraid of what I might see. I could not risk the chance of a direct experience of rejection again.

None of this was on a conscious level at the time, of course, and through my teens, my family life was normal. I loved my mom and dad and continue to hold some of their values dear to me. I don't recall them ever saying an unkind word about one another and they had a good relationship. My mother was on lithium at this point and doing well, but there was always an underlying sadness. How could there not be? But the unwritten family law was *don't upset your mother*. As a consequence, I would spend most of my life trying not to upset *anyone*. People in my experience did drastic things if upset. It was better to absorb all fault and responsibility for anything that might go wrong. It was as if I was, in fact, the "original sin." This fired an intensely independent nature and a detachment from family events where underlying currents were always palpable and unpleasant to me.

It was my instinct as a mother that—unless I consciously shifted—I would either parent the way I was parented or the opposite, neither of which is appropriate for the nurturance of a new soul. I bucked family tradition when it came to refusing having my mother stay with the newborns, purely because I was intent on breaking the influence. I also began my own active healing journey with the assistance of a wonderful Jungian analyst, and one without a prescription pad: Dr. Lois Plumb, the first truly wise woman I met.

In the years after her sister's suicide, my mother was determined to find an answer for her condition and the family dynamic outside the mainstream pathological labeling and medicating. She became

---

[1] Dr. Welch's work has been associated with more extreme practices, which was not my experience at all.

a pioneer in alternative treatments, vitamin therapy and nutrition. Being a nurse, she understood how little the medical world knew of the power of food to heal, nor the affect of good health on our mental outlook. It was a path that was unpopular in those days, when doctors were losing their licenses for referring patients to vitamin or nutrition regimens. Within the family, my mother was looked on as eccentric, and her theories (now mainstream) largely ignored.

I admired my mother hugely for her research and determination. I owe her my own passionate pursuit of wholeness, which has taken me through the constraints of past influences and into an even broader approach to wellbeing. But first I had to take a few detours myself into relationships that let me play out my sense of unworthiness. I attracted just what I expected I deserved, informed by those silent self-saboteurs. I ended up in a miserable, debilitating relationship and making my own lame attempt at suicide, shouting out in the hospital as I was being wheeled to have my stomach pumped that, "Everyone in my family did it!"

When I met George, who would become my husband, I was absolutely astonished at his state of happiness. He was a successful and much revered innovator and fabricator in the construction industry. Even his brothers and friends were happy, and when they gathered, they spoke of wonderful things; accomplishments, challenges—having fun! They were playful and guilt-free. I was twenty-seven and had never seen anything like it. But happiness without judgment was not something I trusted, and being loved for myself was completely beyond comprehension. I did everything I possibly could to dissuade George. One day I finally shouted at his gentleness, "Just wait, when you get to know me, you will hate me too!"

Where this self-loathing came from I can surmise, but why it stuck escapes me except that I never challenged the truth of it directly. Like my mother's eyes, I didn't want to see too deeply. Fortunately I believed what I saw in George's eyes and we had an incredibly happy, creative and constructive life together. His four children from a previous marriage became my family and our two sons were born in the greatest joy and into a loving, extended family. George was a beautiful blend of manliness and sensitivity. A supreme father and adored by all his children. His motto was: "Teach your children self-love and self-esteem, and they will never hurt themselves or another." When our children were born, we engaged a nanny who instantly became a member of the family. We soon determined that, instead of looking after the children, she would look after us so we could devote ourselves wholeheartedly to our sons.

We loved working together, and built and lost and rebuilt several "successful" businesses. My own father, whose family had lost everything in the 1920s, would caution our risk-taking. He would tell of how at ten years old he walked down the steps of the family main street mansion for the last time, holding his mother's hand and carrying only what fitted in their arms; forced to leave the rest of their possessions behind. His words would trigger an anxiety in me that kept me constantly on the lookout for disaster. Indeed, disaster struck and we lost our house during a recession. I would come close to losing our home again after George's death, but the memory of this story became a determinate to change that karma.

The year of the first recession when we lost our business was the same year of my brother's suicide. It was also the year that our nanny, who was the third person to ever hold our firstborn, would die of breast cancer. Our sons were just seven and four. When she first was diagnosed, I panicked. How could I subject my sons to witnessing the death of someone they loved so dearly? There had been entirely too much death and tragedy in my memory. I wanted to save my sons this terrible unhappiness. George, of course, responded from his practical center of love that we were her family and we would care for her, which we did, through three long years of chemotherapy. We were each holding her hand when she died.

I learned a huge lesson as a parent then. Shielding our children from trauma by non-communication, as in my family, or by avoidance, as

I first desired it, deprives our children from learning the very coping and strengthening skills necessary to withstand and manage life's many inevitable challenges and tragedies. It became a period of deep engagement and tender love. It was a crazy time. Our business had been bought and then I was let go, and George was given a severance, as the business became a division of a bigger corporation. There was a recession in the construction industry; George was in his fifties and jobs for entrepreneurs were rare. The construction industry halted and we were about to lose our house.

One day, with nothing to do and no money, the children in school, our beloved nanny dead, George and I took apart some old picture frames and began to sort through boxes of photos. We discovered that all we needed was all we already had, and that was love. The recession lasted several years and we had a few missteps with untrustworthy people offering business opportunities. In one case, our lawyer told us we'd better get out quick—this guy's about to get indicted. We left being owed months of salary, because cons rarely pay their debts. This is when we lost our house.

With the help of George's brother, we bought a smaller house and started over. Eventually, a friendly competitor of George's from the past offered him a partnership in a company. My husband turned the company around from a losing position and several years later it was sold to a large corporation. We invested the proceeds in a country home where I imagined I would stay forever. However, it was during these tentative negotiations that George himself was diagnosed with cancer. He was determined to see the sale through and kept this challenge to himself. It was particularly frightening because George's brother had just been diagnosed with mesothelioma; a very aggressive, environmentally-caused cancer that had taken their older brother just a few years earlier. The three brothers were extremely close and had all worked in the building trade, where asbestos exposure had claimed so many lives.

George's brother spent the final months before his death in a neighboring town, visiting us often with our sons. The two sets of Harding brothers enjoyed cherished evenings sharing growing-up stories, listening to Frank Sinatra and playing billiards by the hour. His death took a terrible toll on George.

George had begun treatment, both traditional and alternative, and we were optimistic. I opened a shop in town and created a website, LightBeam, for holistic lifestyle information and alternative therapies, and George began to plan his consulting business. But two weeks after I opened my shop, George collapsed and was rushed to hospital. He might have died that night, but he lived on: I believe so that our sons (then aged fifteen and eighteen) would have a steadier footing. The next year-and-a-half was a time of equal joy and sorrow; days became precious, and an awakening for me to the next echelon of my journey.

All through my life, I have written to keep my sanity and to find an eloquence and beauty in life just the way it is. I have also relied on a very personal spiritual and interactive relationship with my version of "God," whose description I can only call Love. My family history has shown me that rigorous and moralistic doctrine damages the very loving relationship we desire the most and that is the one with ourselves. My references in this book to Christian stories is with the intent to illuminate the seed of self-love I believe they are meant to convey, rather than the interpretation that love or God is something outside ourselves and a reward for good behavior.

The five years following George's death documented in this book depict the days when I had to find my own compass and navigate out of the forest of the past, and into the clearing of the present. It was the dominion of my spirit over my present circumstances. And it was these very circumstances that provided the means to that clarity, and instilled my will to happiness.

Finding and nurturing the Self inevitably takes us into our own personal ancestry and the influences that unconsciously guide our lives, unfolding as much as our DNA. But—unlike our DNA—we are *not* hardwired by these influences and, by seeing them clearly we begin the journey that brings us into our own light. At least that is what happened to me, and that is what I want to share with these stories.

It's What You Make of It

This book is about self-actualization. It is a singularly individual and independent process and integration. The end point is fairly well described by the title, *Exhilarated Life*. What that means and the evolution to that point are different for me than for you. This is not a well-meaning handbook about how to live happily ever after on an idyllic Greek island. It is about living a life fully realized so that each day—whatever you are doing and wherever you are doing it—is one of health and vitality, intuition and clarity, and the freedom to create every day anew.

The time and experience that these stories span begins in King City, near Toronto, a year after my husband's death, and ends on the island of Aegina five years later, just after securing my Greek visa and embarking on a whole new adventure with my new love, Athan.

I didn't choose this period for its obvious illustration of dramatic change, but for a single pivotal moment just weeks before George's death that shifted my perspective completely and forever, and set these years on an unforeseen trajectory.

In that profound moment, the quest for a deeper knowledge that had fired my whole life transformed from the ineffable to the real. Outwardly I was accomplished, but inwardly I was a quailing mass of insecurity. This changed everything.

It was the moment when George and I accepted that he was about to die, *soon*. I made a promise to help prepare him for that passage. I also vowed to myself, with George as witness, that I would—from that moment—prepare for my own death. Far from being maudlin, it was emancipation: A single beam of light shining through the darkest skies. I would live every day of my life to its fullest.

George's love was an immense love. It flung open the door to life so that I could be all I was meant to be. And, as it turned out, his promise made twenty-seven years before to love me until I loved myself was fulfilled. I was catapulted into that new life and it is for this reason that the collected stories start there.

Too soon to make any kind of sense of it, another love came into my life. I was having dinner with a friend when I mentioned that I had been "out of my body" for so many years, holding the energy through George's illness and death. "I want to dance," I said. "I want to learn Salsa." My friend smiled in an odd way and said, "I'll ask Athan. He has just started Salsa lessons and said he needed a partner." She went on to describe Athan as spiritual, respectful, creative, and one who would never do another harm. Somewhat charismatically, she ended with, "And if anything happens—it happens."

"Nothing is going to *happen*," I rejoined. "My husband just died!"

Athan entered my life as a friend. He took me gently by the hand and together we walked through the years of my mourning. Not long ago, I had the clear awareness that it was not too soon after all, but rather it was the only thing that kept me from going insane with grief. Because he was my friend and of a very loving and open nature, I could share my stories about George. There were many odd similarities and coincidences between the two of them—though a half-generation apart—the same neighborhood growing up, the same homeroom teacher who told them not to sing, but hum the words in glee club, the same fish and chips hangout. And when Athan ordered a hotdog with just mustard and red onions, I knew something was up! But probably more interesting was their dissimilarity. Friends on either side of us would have described Athan and me as chalk and cheese; a most unlikely pairing. But the soul knows a great deal about matches that mere convention misses.

Athan had lost his mother in his teens and so was sensitive to the relationship between my sons and me, respectful of their relationship with their father, and very clear with me he was not an acting replacement. Our friendship had time to grow and eventually flourish to the deep bond of love that it is today. Indeed it was Athan who planted the seed for this book.

The year after George died, it was clear that I could no longer afford to keep our house. It was in the aftermath of the global financial crises that saw real estate drop like a stone. I had moved my fledgling business to a nearby town, which I thought would be more vibrant but that, also, became too costly to maintain. My vision of an Internet-based holistic foundation crashed when it was discovered one of the partners in the website design company had embezzled hundreds of thousands of dollars. I had spent most of my capital on a very comprehensive website, which had never quite worked as designed, and now all the software coders were gone and my site was unusable. I began to take courses in Internet marketing and open source web design. I was determined to see my vision through and ended up wrestling with the web design company to reclaim my own domain name.

In the months before George's death, the roof of our beautiful house had begun to leak badly during a storm and, before the day was over, it had collapsed in several places. Water flooded all floor levels. The damage was everywhere and we called in contractors. We had to move out of the house for a week while they worked. It was as if they sensed the weakness and stress in the household, because acting as one, they tore apart their sections and, when everything was in disarray, demanded more money to finish. We had paid the general contractor in advance and when we challenged him, he walked off the job.

By this time George was in such critical condition that we just left the house unfinished. I would experience the unscrupulousness of contractors again and even end up in court with one. Then I had to use our little remaining capital to fix the house in order to put it on the market the year following George's death. The house would be on the market for two years before its one and only offer.

In the meantime, a wealthy businessman in another city offered me a position. We had met during the negotiations of the sale of our company when George was alive. He had bought a business and said he just knew I would be the perfect one to run it. I was naïve enough to think this was based on my marketing expertise, to which he was witness, rather than my recent widowhood. However, I demurred each succeeding year until the third time he asked and added the offer of partnership. I was on very shaky ground financially, the house still hadn't sold and so leapt at the opportunity.

Athan and I drove the five hundred miles to the city and met a rather surprised president who was told we were there to "turn the place around." I should have known something was up when my "benefactor" offered me a ride and lunged for a kiss in the darkness of the underground parking lot. I overlooked at it as a professional towards a dirty but essentially harmless old man. He had a huge reputation and I trusted his offer of shares in the business. I would find out later when I was nearly broke, having spent all our own money, that he had offered the same thing to three other parties and then went off with his wife and family to his farm in Tuscany, to watch which group won out.

I really started panicking because the bank had not allowed me to mortgage the house earlier on, and now all my capital was gone. I had no income. It was then that a notable artist suggested I would do well as an artists' manager. Again I grasped the opportunity, pitting my marketing skills, confidence and need to succeed against more sound judgment of avoiding the inherently quixotic art market during a global financial meltdown.

It was at this frantic juncture that I almost made the fateful mistake of encumbering my house with a second mortgage, which most certainly would have ended up with the house in receivership, and me walking away holding my sons' hands with only what our arms could carry. I had my hand on the phone when, in a flash of instinct, I said, "No!" I also said no to my agent, who recommended I drop the price. I knew from experience the kind of people that are attracted to the duress of others, and I wasn't going to let myself in for that humiliation. As if the universe had heard, the house sold within weeks at nearly the asking price—and for the highest price ever recorded in our neighborhood.

But I wasn't out of the woods yet. I was so relieved to call the bank to tell them the good news and arrange bridge financing to hire a moving firm, and for a down payment on a rental or purchase. To my astonishment, the bank refused. Once again I had encountered someone who enjoyed wielding power over others. I had a house with hardly any mortgage on it, with a sale ready to close in six weeks and absolutely no money except for food. I was behind in taxes and owed on the utilities bill. That was it! I was done with being the victim of the lousiest kind of human nature. I wrote an email to the CEO of the bank with the subject title, "Slow bludgeoning by bank employee," and detailed at length how the global banking system in general and this bank in particular was responsible for the gradual demise of my personal financial position. Within hours I had a response from a VP and the landscape of my life changed dramatically.

I secured the bridge financing, the sale of the house closed, all debts were paid off and then I faced the next hurdle—where to now? Athan (a creative marketing entrepreneur) and I decided to build on our efforts in the art world, and rented a place in the cultural epicenter of Toronto. We had made meager inroads in innovative art marketing and sales in an industry that it is an understatement to call "quirky." We even created a publishing company and published several art-related books. Along with wonderfully enduring friendships and associations with most in our creative world, we encountered corrosive egos and again found someone we trusted acting behind our backs. Instead of just parting ways, the aftermath was vicious. It was a costly mistake both financially and emotionally. People say, "Never do business with friends," yet I disagree. I just became much more discerning in whom I call friend and with whom I do business.

I learned a vital lesson from these two characters, consecutive as they were at a time of my vulnerability. It was this: When people acquire power either by wealth or fame, they are often driven by some lack in their own life, and wielding power over others is usually compensatory. Those who are attracted to perceived safety under his or her graces are easily manipulated and exploited. Like any good survival show, the cross purposes of all those who would gain favor are a tangle of competing and desperate forces. Pitting one against the other and watching the play is sustenance for these types of ego. It was only in blushing retrospect that I saw the game and my place in it. I was naively drawn in by promises that neither could keep. It was not in their nature, nor was it their purpose.

Ultimately our successes in the art world were meaningful and fulfilling. However, my heart had gone out of the challenge and a whole new adventure lay on the horizon. One where I would gather up all forces and influences, lessons and skills, and find myself worthy of my own professional attention. This book is a result of that trust and evolving self-belief.

I offer these stories as a bridge of understanding so that you can see beyond where you are now. There is no single book or workshop or pill or incantation that cuts out the process. The process is where you get to love yourself just the way you are. Embrace it. Embrace your Self.

I have deliberately placed these stories in the chronology in which they were written because it shows a certain progression. On the other hand, as I have worked on this compilation I have found that some of these were letters to my future self, offering a map of sorts. Your wisdom is within you now. All I offer is a light to show you the way. Use this book as a companion; one that you can call on anytime and open at any page. I was guided as I wrote and trust you will hear the words that you need to hear at any given moment.

This is by no means a claim that this book has mystical properties, but a conviction gained from experience that, as we clarify our intention to self-actualization, the synchronicity of the universe conspires to help us in the most subtle but sublime ways. Songs, a chance meeting, random words at a moment of need will resonate and assure you that you are indeed "no less than the trees and the stars; you have a right to be here."[2]

Happiness is a state that raises the vibrancy of the physical body and lets our true nature shine. You are the spark from the brilliant flame of all that has ever been created and all that may ever be created. When you know that for yourself, you will find your place in the world and life will be sweet, happy and, well, *exhilarated!*

---

2 Desiderata, Max Ehrmann, 1927

Gathering the Pearls

Athens

Opening the Shutters

Letting in the light.

In the apartment we have rented in Athens, the ceilings are fourteen feet high. Around the upper reaches is a two-foot band of sky blue clasped between white cornice and molding. Pale sunlight-yellow cascades to the floor. The herringbone wood cuts diagonal lines in dark and light shades of honey. A long, low leopard print sofa and great, weathered dining table that serves as my desk dominate the room, rendering it simultaneously regal and amusing. A chair covered in paper leaves from a stage play of *Midsummer Night's Dream* completes the whimsy. Two sets of French doors stand shoulder to shoulder and let the morning light flood in while the birdsong sails in on the wings of the breezes that blow down from the Acropolis.

We are not yet a week in Athens, but already the crumbling of my old life has begun, as I knew it would. I didn't know how things would shift, but what was started a few short months ago—when I cast off the bowlines of permanent home—I held close to me until I felt I was in an environment ancient enough to imbue my transition with wisdom and strength.

Here I am not home, but I have arrived at a place where I will stay and write. The lure of the familiar and routine is no longer drawing on me to be busy and distracted. Here, I must make sense of the foolhardiness of putting all my worldly goods in a storage locker and getting on a plane to a place where I do not speak the language. My soul seems to know what is going on because I have never been so at ease or slept as well as I have in this place. But my mind is still saying, "What the…?"

We all make choices, and I now choose to be who I am without apology. However, it seems that to reveal my Self to myself, I must first let go of everything that does not become me. So, dark in the recesses of my locker in Toronto, stuff awaits my return. I will look with fresh eyes and choose again when it is time to make a new home. But that time is not now, and I have all that I require in a suitcase in the next room. Oh yes, and in the one person whom I trust to share this passage with me: Athan.

Athan can be incredibly annoying because he holds a mirror to me that I often resist looking into. I allow him to expose me to myself because behind the mirror are amber-green eyes so full of love and tenderness that my heart quiets, and I can look without embarrassment. Ironically, I resist looking at my strengths and loveliness with vigor equal to my resistance to looking at my weaknesses. Actually, what I just described is my only weakness, and I think it is common to us all. We rarely see our loveliness, and we witness our flaws as the foundation of our incomplete Self. There are no real weaknesses in any of us, just the unwillingness to accept ourselves as we are, *now*, and to see our challenges of Self as we play out our lives. Working through the frustrations and obstacles to our inner happiness and fulfillment *is* Life. It is not about reaching goals—financial, social or spiritual—it is about *being*. The accouterments of prestige or wealth will come—or not. The deciding factor to their showing up in our lives is our inherent aspiration.

Many wish they could win the lottery, but a simple question will reveal the truth of this desire: What would you do with a million dollars? After the new house and the trip to the Caribbean and a few things that deteriorate over time, we have pretty much expended our material dreams. The two riches that really hold any lasting quality, and we mistakenly imagine might be purchased with money are freedom and love. Those do not come from the outside but from the deep well within. Freedom is the letting go of anything that keeps you from simply walking in another direction.

Love begins with you, for the you that you are right now, in your fullness and in your flawed-ness. Love is like water. When it is poured, it finds every chink, fissure, and hollow, and fills it to overflowing. You cannot guide the path of water; water finds its own path—and so does love. When you pour love out of your deepest heart, you stand in the center of the fountain of Life itself.

I came here to Europe to find out which parts of me were real and which parts of me were habit, or derived from wanting to please others, or from whispers from past generations that had nothing to do with me.

A friend commented to me once over a chatty lunch, "You, of all people I know, have done the most work on yourself, and yet you are still like *this*!" She was wondering why I still hadn't "arrived." It made me wonder, too, as I described the onionskin aspect of being revealed to one's Self. I no longer wonder. I know. My zeal for self-awareness through psychotherapy, Reiki, yoga, and all kinds of therapies and practices only shone the light on the deep kernel that I had constructed my life around: My innate unworthiness. The unworthiness was real. It was a shell as hard and tight as an oyster that held within it the pearl of my own divine essence.

Oh, I've chipped away at it over the decades. I've learned through relationships—business and personal; 'good' and 'bad'. I've learned through raising two sons and know that our children are our teachers. Parenting reveals our Selves to ourselves most clearly if we accept the true nature of the reciprocal dynamic. I learned through the death of my husband, whose love was like a fortress of protection. When he died, I found that my foundations crumbled because they were built on his truth of me, not my own truth of myself. Life with George felt better because I could quiet my nasty little voice when I looked into his eyes, rested in his arms, and lived in our home together. I was loved, and that was enough.

As surely as a single drop of rain will find its way to the ocean and ascend once more, we all long to find our way to our true source, and that is Love. It is what drives us. Where we get messed up is in withholding Love from ourselves until we have achieved some perceived right to worthiness. We look into a mirror darkly, and our reflection is obscured by what we are looking for. The body? The intellect? The house? The clothes? The title? The youth? The spirituality? Many religions tell us that, at some distant time, presumably after death, we will see ourselves as God or Creation sees us. We will know our divinity essentially when it is too late for it to do us—or this world—any real good. Is it any wonder we are confused? We have to claim divine eyes right now and see ourselves clearly as perfected spirits unfolding through human experience.

I think we are living in a cosmic car rally, and all the clues are there in ancient scriptures and myths, and also in the abundant metaphors that nature offers us. We are driving too fast to read the signs correctly. We think we get the gist of it, and off we go over the hills of distraction, looking for something that we will not find. The answer is right here, and it is the love you have for yourself as you are right now. Here and now are the only compass points by which we are truly able to navigate. All else is in the abundant play of infinite possibility. If I stop writing and go for a walk, what series of incidents will play out and differ from if I stop writing, go make coffee, and see what Athan is working on in the other room?

Since I have chosen to continue writing, I am moved to say that—knowing that we exist in a pool of infinite possibility, countless choices that lead to countless times a zillion outcomes—we have no concrete past or certain future. We have illusions of past events and probabilities for future outcomes. In the one glittering moment when I discovered that someone I thought had loved me all my life proved he didn't, and, in fact, he hated me passionately, all was made clear to me, and the past as I knew it was dissolved. I am no longer committed to my own illusion and now am free. Actually, I was always free from a past that has infinite subjective versions, just as you are.

So, what now? I am committed to my own "now." I am writing the book with which I have teased my soul for decades by writing snippets on a blog, in articles, short children's stories, or poetry. I have let my truths dribble instead of surge out of me, which left me anemic and looking for fulfillment elsewhere. I am okay with writing and not knowing whether it will be relevant to any other person. It is relevant to me, and that is enough. There was a time when George said, "If you have one flaw, it is that you want to change the world." My response at the time was, "Yes, and?" Now I know what he meant, and I no longer want to change the world. I can't, anyway. All I can do is change myself and adjust my own bearings until I am sailing with benevolent winds on a sea of happiness.

I wanted to change the world because I hurt so badly. Each time I found a healing salve through meditation, Reiki, or whatever, I wanted to shout it out so that everyone would be saved from hurt. But it is our struggle with the constraints of our acquired roles and relationships, the abrasion of conflict within ourselves and with others, that gives us the strength and patience to emerge from the enclosure of our little self into the full color and freedom of our larger Self. Just like the butterfly, we need the process itself to gain our radiance.

Of course, not everyone wants to be saved. Not everyone wants to ascend. Not everyone questions the meaning of life or desires any kind of answer. Lots of people are okay just being okay.

All I am doing is polishing my own eyes from the inside so that I see the gorgeous world in its infinite unfolding of creation, the source of which is pure Love. This is the love that cradles both dark and light. We come to our own self-love by peeling, chipping, dissolving or bludgeoning our way through the layers of untruths that disguise our true nature.

No relationship or experience is without merit in contributing to this quest. However, each relationship and experience can more deeply encrust our true nature if we remain unconscious. I know. I spent a lifetime trying to please others in an effort to overcome the inner bleat of unworthiness. The voice I discovered was not my own, nor a higher guiding wisdom, but rose from unexamined messages of generations.

This morning I have opened the shutters and opened the doors. The spring breeze is cool but promises a warming sun. Over the rooftops and high above, I glimpse the crumbling but majestic monument to the Muses on Filopappos Hill and know what has brought me here.

Canada to Greece
via Hollywood

Rose Petals

The Little Drama vs. the Big Picture.

Yesterday I made love to my home. I reclaimed her as my sanctuary. I got down on my hands and knees and actually reached under furniture, damp dusted the underside of things where the dog hair clung, carefully rewound the Christmas tree lights, dragged the tree outside, vacuumed the pine needles from under the carpet, and put the gasping poinsettias outside to "go to sleep."

There are two significant aspects of this; one is that I normally mutter and spit through a perfunctory swiping of the floor—gathering the tumbleweeds of pet hair, and not quite reaching the corners. I usually make a joke that the maid will get the rest—but I am she…and well, you just can't get good help these days. The second is that I am putting my home in order after the first Christmas and New Year since my beloved husband George's death, last February.

Three weeks ago I was ready to bolt. I was going to take my sons to a beach somewhere and let the holiday roll right on past. It was my younger son who stopped me in my tracks. He said, "I don't know why you have a problem with Christmas. Last year wasn't our best Christmas, for sure, but this is our home and this is where we should be." In those words and in his wise young eyes was the absolute spirit of George. It is just what he would have said. I hugged him in relief for his clarity and the three of us chose to celebrate the season by having a holiday much more joyful and healing than sad.

On Christmas Eve a year ago I knew that George was going to die. On Christmas Day at 11:00PM a 20lb turkey, stuffing and vegetables were dumped into a green garbage bag—no one could eat. At 3:00AM the day after Boxing Day, my older son, Nick, helped me maneuver George into the car, and I drove my husband to the hospital, where he stayed the week. He wanted so much to be home for New Year's that he was released that afternoon. We no sooner got home than we realized it was a mistake.

As the clock ticked toward midnight, New Year's Eve, George and I sat in the emergency room; George in a wheelchair, silent and still, enduring God knows what kind of pain, and me breathing and praying. Our two sons, aged twenty and seventeen, were out at celebrations. I wouldn't call them until after midnight to tell them I had brought their dad back to the hospital. They had been so relieved when he had been allowed to come home just that afternoon. But wait, that isn't the point of this story.

That part is the Little Drama as opposed to the Big Picture, as I have come to view Life over the past several years. My good friend calls it the "Epic Story." Like the Iliad. The one that is truly our path to God, which in my view is manifest in self-actualization, the path of love seeking love. It is the divine blueprint of All That We Can Be. That path leads us right through the minefield of the small self with all its fears and rages, and life and death dramas, to our Greater Self—the poet, teacher or leader who resides in the heart of God or divine creation.

Here there is no death. Or rather death has no "sting." There is only love—in its many and glorious forms. As we are birthed into this world, live and sooner or later die out of this world, we can be carried through our darkest nights on the grace of this knowing, or be badly bruised on the harshness of a "real" and physical world. It actually becomes a conscious choice over which only we have control.

I cannot trivialize the illness and death of my husband, the father of my sons, my business partner, mentor, lover, and soul mate. "George and Marilyn" was a phrase. For twenty-seven years we worked together, played together, had lunch together, shopped together, and on the way home in separate cars chatted on our cells to one another. We always had something to talk about. We rarely argued. We loved one another deeply and always wanted what was best for the other. We were only ever apart three or four times in more than a quarter century.

Was I afraid? Yes, I was terrified. I look back and realize I had bargained with God and offered to endure years of a million daily fears in exchange for the One Big One.

Was I sad? Yes, many nights I lay on our bedroom floor and wailed in the middle of the night, mindless in sorrow.

Was I angry? You bet. I hated the arrogance of doctors, the soullessness of CAT scans, the iniquity of the body. I was bloody outraged that my husband was to die. I wasn't ready!

Did I suffer? In the sleepless nights and the numbed out days when I couldn't fix what was broken, yes.

But so what? It all happened anyway—whether I liked it or not.

What emerged from the depths of my experience were a series of lessons about life and death. Really about life, mostly. They are a mere handful of truths that will help us live life more fully, prepare for our own death more objectively and accept the death of those we love. Death is just the context for living our life. We are all going to die, one way or another, sooner or later. We all know this but continue to act surprised or betrayed when the end befalls us or one we love. There are no untimely deaths. Cancer, car accident, or crib death is merely part of the script. We all have an exit ticket.

There is a purpose to every single human life and how we express that to its fullest is our job on this planet. To the extent that we fulfill that mandate, the easier it will be for us to let go of the physical world and give ourselves over.

There is a saying that a good life means a good death. To my mind a "good" life does not mean one of perfection—pleasing God in our flawless following of rules, but of being *real* in all its darks and lights and striving. When we embrace this truth, we express our divinity in being God's hands, eyes, mouth, ears, heart—healer, artist, teacher, counselor, lover—whatever.

The irony of all this is that I live in a world of healers—spiritual, energetic, natural. A world of miracles. In fact it is my business. After we sold our company and retired, George helped me realize my dream. In July 2005, two weeks after I opened my boutique dedicated to the healing and creative arts, George collapsed and was rushed to hospital. He had a tumor from prostate cancer that had shut down his kidneys, he needed fourteen liters of blood, and he nearly died. The oncologist refused to take him on as a patient because she said there was nothing she could do. His urologist said he wouldn't live until Christmas (2005), and he would spend the rest of his life dependent on dialysis.

George lived another eighteen months. He did it for me and our two sons, his family, and many others whose lives he touched during that time. I thought he was going to be my poster boy for miracles. How could the husband of one in the healing world die of the nastiest of illnesses—cancer?

But George did die. And in that passing emerged a profoundly beautiful love story. For in that final walk on Earth together, George, always my protector, led me through the fire of my greatest fears, and in return, I had the privilege of looking deeply into his eyes as he passed through the veil so he would not be afraid. From that moment the life and death drama of every day fell away and I witnessed my own soul's journey.

I have lived my life in pursuit of the spiritual. I have prayed for clarity and understanding. I was certain that as I prayed for God's Will to be done, that if I was really good and fulfilled my guidance in building this business around living life authentically and spiritually, I would be rewarded by my husband's miraculous cure. How else could I really interpret his illness?

As it happened, something was lost in my interpretation. When I surrendered (small 's') to God's Will, I sensed this voice saying, "Are you sure?" and I answered, "Yep, yep, yep!" because, of course, I thought I knew what that meant. But what God really meant was that I would have to go where I dreaded more than anywhere on earth—and that was to the hospital. In this case, forty-two hours in the emergency section where George, awaiting medication, rocked back and forth on his gurney in pain and I sat on an overturned barf bowl for hours on end. God's Will also meant that I would ultimately have to give up my beloved when in my heart of hearts I knew he could have been "healed." This is where I learned that healing does not always mean living.

To some I have shown strength or courage, but the truth is strength comes through surrender. In surrendering to what is, we can then look to what we need to lift us up and move us through a difficult passage. This is where I can gratefully acknowledge the cast of hundreds who helped me—and George and family—by word or deed, practice, therapy or healing to take Life in hand and really live it…to death.

This is the part I want to share. The circumstances of the Little Drama are the tools for the Big Picture and serve only as the flash cards of greater meaning and purpose.

Yesterday, I plucked some faded roses from the Christmas centerpiece on the dining table. I was about to put them in the recycling bin, but instead to honor George (who never threw flowers in the garbage), I went out on the deck and, opening each dead rose one at a time, strewed them across the snow. The crisp brown outer petals fell away in my hands, and within the bud, deep pink silken petals unfurled. Snowflakes and rose petals swirled in the air, then cascaded to the ground and rested there. As I looked out the window and saw the graceful pattern they left, it was a message that, like the roses, there is no death—just transformation and beauty when we look through the eyes of Love.

My Mother Didn't Cry—She Wept

How to let go of depression and other saboteurs of happiness.

The muses, for me, are like a child, predawn, on Christmas morning. They stand quietly near my bed, lift an eyelid and whisper, "Are you awake?" I roll over and try to ignore the gentle prodding and then there will be a voice in my mind. Some image—grouping of words—an inspiration of something that might be shared. I promise myself I will remember it all in the morning. But no. It is now that the phrases begin to tumble forth and, well, I might as well swing out of bed and follow the little voice nudging me up the stairs. I can nap later.

So here I am in a predawn, hushed house. The fire is burning and the Tiffany lamp casts a warm, colorful glow. Living with two young musicians, it is not easy to find the house quiet until very late or, in this case, very early. Even the dogs, Zoe, the Golden Retriever and Skye, the Siberian Husky, are too deeply asleep to leave my room where "all us girls" bunk down each night.

What has me awake? What is it I want to share with you? What is so urgent? Well, I want to tell you about happiness. How to coax it into your life so it's not just a once in a while (got the promotion—won the lottery—just engaged) kind of thrill, but an abiding joyful state of being. Once it underlies all the inevitable detritus—let's call it garbage—that we might be called to endure, we become like boats buoyant on happiness, and more easily navigate this often tough and heavy world.

If I want to talk about happiness, why do I begin with the title about weeping? Because Life is a walk we take alone and it can be sad. We drop in at birth and ease out at death, and in between we *à la main* left and *à la main* right with any number of characters, lovers, cheats, family, betrayers, gurus and frauds. Each one teaches us something about ourselves and, dammit, the toughest teachers bring us our brightest lessons—closer to happiness. Some of these lessons we can experience on a higher level and see their importance, but many have swooped in and taken us at a vulnerable, unguarded moment. They have embedded themselves deeply in our soul, and our mind just doesn't pick up on them. These experiences are barbed with sharp emotion—usually shame, vulnerability, or guilt—and because they don't make themselves clear, they attract similar experiences. We are left wondering why we keep picking the wrong kind of guy, people cheat us, or we become ill.

My Life work—or vision—has been a force of nature beyond my choice: To stop the pervasive sadness that wove its way through the family tapestry. How far back does it go? It doesn't matter. I can swing a cat (gently) and touch a batch in my immediate family who suffer in a way that makes their lives go out of ease and balance. Responses include illness, depression, self-destructive behavior, even suicide. I include myself in that. Are we any different from every family? Any individual? No. When we live in "dis"ease even joyful events are only fleeting. We catch glimpses of a happiness we desire but cannot sustain.

Global cataclysms, man-made or natural, send shock waves through the world as we know it, but they are not separate from us. They affect us directly or peripherally, but they rise up from each one of us—from our collective unhappiness and out-of-ease-ness.

Healing begins in our own hearts. Our own minds. Our own bodies. Our souls. We can't ask for or expect peace in the world when we can't claim it for ourselves. We can't ask for or expect happiness for our children if we do not model it ourselves. We can't expect an earth in balance if we cannot first heal ourselves.

My mother didn't cry—she wept. When I was little—nine or so—I would climb into bed with her when my dad was on a business trip. In the night, as I snuggled into her side, I would become aware of the deep shudders that she tried to keep still and then I would feel the wetness of her face as the tears cascaded endlessly, in silent heaving. I know now some of her past and how it could cause this sadness. I didn't know her future then, but she would have more to weep for.

I too have wept in the night. Overcome by fears and worries—"nameless dreads", as a friend used to call these night thoughts. I have invited the dreads into my waking life. They were real. Loss of income, house, betrayals, death, suicide. Lotsa junk. Keeping my chin up, ever plunging on, stepping over broken businesses, promises, lives. What are ya gonna do? S**t happens.

Well, stop crying about it for one. And then start dumping out. I like the image of defragging a computer. When I finally discovered the "clean up the disc" button, a little box came up with stripes of all colors. They represented whole files and "broken" files. Whole files function and the fragmented files (red) are broken bits of files deleted, but not all gone. They gum up the works. Slow things down and cause all sorts of problems—way out of my scope to describe or fix—except to defrag. We don't even know they are in there yet they act like sticks in our spokes. Things function after a fashion, but nothing really works well and smoothly, and every once in a while—crash!

For me—as much as I am keen to be computer competent—noodling "in there" is like doing brain surgery with salad forks. It may not be something you want to manage unsupervised, not at least, until you become a little more familiar. Healing the soul is much like that. Healing the soul is vitally important, as it is the seat of expressing all our life force through body, mind, and spirit.

If you want health and happiness, vitality, courage and peace—begin on the inside. So many therapies are amazing facilitators for this task. Bodywork by a conscious therapist becomes soul work. Simple gentle touch by a caring person can pop open a soul like a ripe milkweed pod. When someone puts their hands on your body, they plunge their reach deep into your subtle energies. Even sex as an act of incredible intimacy is a blunt object (no pun intended) compared to the incisive effect of soul or energy therapy. It is very effective and very sensitive.

Many who suffer from the effects of a discordant soul may be reluctant to "do the work" because they fear reliving what has caused them enormous pain in the first place. But unlike psychotherapy—although that too has its place—there are many alternative therapies that are more efficient and effective. Once limiting emotions and beliefs are released, life events and circumstances almost immediately shift to a more fulfilling, constructive and effortless synchronicity. Each time I shed another layer, I see the result reflected in life experience and wish I had let go of it sooner!

Enlightenment isn't just for monks. It is for all of us who choose to "lighten up." Defrag, drop the load, clear the clutter of unpleasant, unproductive memories and emotions. They just sabotage your happiness. Take charge of your own happiness—it is your right! And weep no more.

Eating Artichokes Whole is Prickly

How to take the good of Life's lessons and dispose of the rest.

Yes, I've done this too—eaten the artichoke that is. I was nineteen at the time and in a very elegant restaurant in Montreal. I was at university on the East coast and very attached to my boyfriend in Toronto. He was my first love and very handsome—like a young Michael Caine—actually even Michael Caine was young then, too. I would send soppy letters of longing home and he would respond with a carton of cigs and a Ziggy Stardust album closing with the line: "Wish you were there," which was his way of saying be where you are.

That past September my folks packed up my big, blue steamer trunk in the car for us to travel that part of Canada and get me settled into the residence at Acadia University in Nova Scotia. My boyfriend waved me off with the advice to have the time of my life, which was his way of saying that is what he intended to do.

I finally took his advice and that is when, while watching the Canadian Varsity Football on TV, he happened to glimpse me in the stands wrapped in a big, red plaid blanket with a hunk of a mountain man from New Hampshire! Who knew? Anyway, true to the nature of many men, when something looks like it might go missing it becomes more valuable and desired. Along came his letter with a ticket to Montreal and a heartfelt plea "Wish you were here." Like many young women, I finally got what I asked for. And it wasn't what I wanted.

Anyway, Montreal is Montreal, exotic in its French Canadian culture and I thought it would make a nice change for him to pitch me for a bit, and then I could ditch him. So off I went on my post romantic adventure. I only remember two things: His very satisfying suffering that I was no longer "his," and the feel of a slice of artichoke in my mouth. There I was being all haughty and cool with my newfound power of resistance, and suddenly I was contending with a mouthful of sharp, hairy cardboard! I instantly knew I had made a gaff—or how could artichokes be so popular? But it wasn't a moment to laugh off my own silliness, a very useful trait that I have since developed. I can't honestly remember how I discretely disposed of the mess in my mouth, but I do recall the lesson: Swallow the good stuff and spit out the rest.

All too often we bite off something in a job, relationship or other commitment and it doesn't feel so good. But this much I will guarantee: You are being called to learn something about yourself. If you are cheated, you can learn discernment. If you are betrayed, you can learn forgiveness. If you have been humiliated, you can learn courage. Strengthening character is like any muscle. You have to hit the weights until you get strong.

Fitness clubs garner the greatest income from unused memberships. It is not human nature to seek out the difficult and discipline ourselves. We only "get religion" when we've gone too far. The dress doesn't fit and the party is next week or we have a heart attack. Life in its natural yearning and push to higher evolution provides the impetus for we humans who would avoid discomfort. We could develop strength, courage, peace, happiness, health and vitality by choice—many do—but more don't. Life crooks its finger and beckons to us. We, in response say, "Who me?" and look over our shoulder. "Yes," Life says, "it is time to learn courage—you will need it later," and sends a bully to kick sand in your face—someone for you to stand and face in your own goodness and power.

There is a lovely children's story by Neale Donald Walsch, and I paraphrase like mad, but it goes something like this: A little soul had never been to Earth and was hearing stories about the delight of forgiveness.

"God! I want to learn forgiveness! Can I go? Pleeeease?"

"Okay," said God, "but you can't go alone."

"I'll go with Little Soul," said Little Soul's best friend.

"Goody!" said Little Soul.

"But you know, Little Soul," said Best Friend, "when we get there I will have to do something to you for you to forgive. When I do—just remember who I am."

I love this story because it so simply illustrates that the people and circumstances in our lives help us to be all that we can be. We all are born with our unique and fabulous mix of talents, competencies and desires. Our potential is boundless and only diminished by the limitations of our own mind, and by our latent abilities, talents and strengths. So many whisperings by teachers, parents, and sadly our religions, form our expectations long before we are of discerning age. As we grow, we grow according to the expectation of others. Sometimes—often—we are unaware of the underlying sabotaging script to our own powerful potential.

That is when Life steps in. List all the qualities of Life you think are desirable. Happiness is top on my list because it means all else is in harmony. I don't mean manic happiness, as in "I laugh in the face of danger!" but a "default" setting to happiness that ensures that I can ride the waves of joy and sorrow with equal grace. So what are the qualities you desire most to form your life experience? Courage? Creativity? Vitality? Peace? Bliss? Now think on the various circumstances and experiences of your life, and see how each might have offered you an opportunity to achieve a measure of those values.

This is not the same as getting slugged in the head and deciding never to venture back to that neighborhood. It is not about taking the tough stuff on the chin and sighing in resignation, saying, "I know there is a lesson in this for me." It's not Life saying, "I'm going to teach you a lesson you'll never forget!" It is not about punishment in any way. It is all about *freedom*.

Freedom to be exactly who you are in all your creative abandon and joyful expression—as a dancer, an artist, a salesperson, a parent or a bank manager! If you are just exactly who you are, you can never get it wrong! No one can criticize or judge you because you are being a perfect expression of your whole potential. Sometimes we hang on to relationships, jobs or possessions because we have a misguided notion that to let go is failure. But sometimes those things have fulfilled their purpose in our lives and can be discarded.

The beginning of wisdom and self-actualization is to get this. It helps you understand the notion that we are to see the divine in all people. Seeing the divine doesn't mean a rapist isn't a rapist—really. It means that there is a deeper soul agreement at work that is moving toward consciousness and evolution. If you balk at the example of rapist, just remember that Life as creator is eternal and infinite. There is no death—it only exists on the physical plane. There is nothing that can truly harm the soul. "No fire can burn it. No water can wet it." Life will use even death to open our eyes to the beauty of our full human potential.

When you know this you will have a very different perspective of a difficult passage or person. What part of you is better for this experience? Which of the qualities that you most desire are closer to you now? Now the important part is to take the gem and drop the painful experience. You may never forget it, but it no longer has an emotional hook to trip you up. Continuing to be outraged by a painful betrayal is to stay heavily attached to something that has outlived its use to you. Keep the lesson of discernment; trust in your own intuition (that likely warned you but you didn't listen), and find the courage to call it like it is.

The emotions of the hairy, prickly stuff of Life experience are:

resentment, guilt, fear, anger, rage, depression, trepidation, self-consciousness, doubt and anxiety. Do you really want to carry these heavy feelings with you? Are these the energies that you want attracting circumstances and people into your life? It's not tough to let these lower energies go. The way is simple: You can't focus on two things at the same time. Be conscious of your thoughts and choose to enjoy the gem. It's valuable and you earned it! Then you can relish the lovely, fleshy, nutty green pleasure of eating artichokes and toss the hairy bits and prickles in the compost heap—they're just fertilizer!

I Planted a Flower but Desired a Fruit

Does your life reflect your heart's desires?

Whenever I hear the phrase, "You reap what you sow," I picture my Aunt Myrtle's piercing brown-black eyes and her mouth clamped shut in final punctuation. The meaning was unmistakable. It was all about punishment for misdeeds. And, man—I was guilty all day long! I didn't say thank you. I didn't smooth the pleats in my kilt before I sat down. I cried when she made me cut my hair in a "pixie" style. I refused to eat her lumpy, burned gravy and it was decades before I ate parsnips again (who boils them?). I was ungrateful, unmanageable, and "too moody for my own good."

It hardly matters now when I reflect that she was probably flung into an emergency, looking after her brother's three children when their mom lost her grip and ended up in a psychiatric hospital. Aunt Myrtle died many years later but before I was old enough to understand her or begin to forgive her. Instead she just lodged herself as my inner voice of critical reason, caution, and propriety. She doesn't always ask permission to opine, but I have gotten firmer in telling her to button it. Before you think I am hearing voices and am ready for the bin myself, let me just say that Aunt Myrtle is merely a handy reference for the unexamined script that ran my life for decades.

We often don't know where we got this sense of unworthiness. We might blame our genes—but this is not in our physical cells. This current runs through our emotions—the electrical charges. Can you feel it? I know I can right now as I remember. It reaches right across my chest and grips my shoulders. I'm sure this is the path it took in my little body before it reached up my neck into my face as a blush. Then the tears of anger and humiliation. Potent mix! I was so often embarrassed or ashamed for just being me. I was never even really naughty. What a waste!

So what happened then? My mother came home (after five years) and we cobbled our broken family back together with the tacks of blunted emotions. Were we different from other families? Only by degree or circumstance. I grew up in a neighborhood where the parents of my friends had been in concentration camps and lost entire families. There's another thing—I didn't deserve to be upset or petulant in the face of real tragedy. But that's the point, isn't it? Gilda Radner's wonderful character, Roseanne Roseannadanna, said it best: "It's always something!"

It really doesn't matter what "something" hems us in, be it horrendous circumstances or misguided goodness. If the bird of our soul is caged then it cannot fly. Often, long after the captors of our spirit are gone, we hobble along like the ladies of ancient China on their tiny bound feet. We have embraced our own crippled nature as if, in its familiarity, it is who we really are. The tether, long since severed in the physical, continues to bind us emotionally. The result is we transfer the power of the captors of our spirit onto other external "authority."

That could continue to be our parents: "Forget being a musician—get a proper job." Our teachers: "You'll never be a painter if you don't paint this way." Our religion: "You'll never get to heaven if you do that." Our lovers: "You sound so lame when you sing!" So we cut and prune ourselves and launch into the grown-up world—right into the hands of the media. Too old! Too fat! Too bald! This car! That house! Our beer! We are so out of touch with who we really are, we grasp at anything that makes us believe we might fly. Viagra. Botox. Zoloft. Hummer. Versace. Smirnoff.

So. We plant a flower. Flowers are good. Everybody likes them. Can't go wrong with that. Except, as beautiful as they are, and as sweet as they smell, it is not what we really want. Flowers stand apart from us in a vase. To be observed and admired.

It is not a flower that can satisfy our longing. Our desire is for deeper sustenance. What our soul craves is a ripe fruit. Split open. Seeds and juice spilling into our mouth and overflowing down our chin. Messy but nourishing. Satisfying. Pleasurable. Succulent. Oh, but isn't it a little embarrassing to be so outspoken about such sensuality? Isn't it wrong or impolite to say what we really desire? How we desire to feel? How we desire to be loved? Haven't we been taught that what we really desire—our scruffy sweater, our ten-year-old car, our familiar and cozy house, a simple job that leaves our mind free, whatever—is not what we should want?

Hmm. It's all a little confusing isn't it? Lately there are more books, movies, CDs and seminars about the law of attraction. It's absolutely true. But the problem is we are attracting from the want and not the desire. Big difference! We want to fit in. We want to achieve. We want a yacht. We want a Mercedes. We want a villa on the beach. We want to win the lottery. We want a flower. The trouble with wants is their satisfaction is fleeting. They fill us up but we are soon hungering again. Wants are the constant distractors from our soul's desires. Wants always lie on the horizon of life. In the distance. As the want—the car, the house, the lover—comes closer, we pluck it up and see that the horizon is ever before us. And what is on the far horizon, beckoning? A faster car. A bigger house. A younger lover.

What then? Well, back to Aunt Myrtle, fruit and purple velvet shoes. Oh, didn't I tell you about the purple velvet shoes? They had straps that could slip down behind the heel and big purple jewels on the front. They also had a gold lining. I loved them! I'm sure they were pronounced gaudy and unsuitable. Anyway, I got saddle shoes instead and, at five, had to learn to color white shoe polish inside the lines with that blunt little dauber thing—without spilling the whole bottle all over the newspaper—oh yeah, I did. Inevitably there were unsightly smears on the navy bits; testament to my clumsiness. That alone has stunted me in ways I fear to think! In rebelliousness, I would scuff my toes all the way to school. What a terror!

Forgive me: I digress. Back to desires. What are they and how do we know one from a want? Well, desires are yearnings of the soul for expression. Yearnings to connect with others who share similar desires. Even the simplest stroking of a desire has it purring in the heart as contentment. Desires are born of love and thrive in love. Our heart's desires are Life's yearning to express itself through our own unique and particular expression of it. We pick up a brush, put it to canvas and feel the color even as we see it. We hum a tune we've never heard before and a song is born. We take off the suit of career and lie back to birth a child. We are released from an illness and devote our life to healing. We step out of the corporate harness and craft our own business. We sail around the world in a boat or on the Internet. What we do makes a difference because we do it from love. And the joy of it all? When we act from love we are free!

In expressing our heart's desires, we draw in the very love of Self that has been our nameless longing, forever. As we fill with self-love we embody self-respect and self-esteem. With these qualities we will never harm another or ourselves. We will grow in confidence, creativity, and reverence for others and the world we live in. We will know peace within because there will be no other voice of authority but Love. That expression might be as an engineer or a dancer, a parent or a bank manager. Desires by nature are nurturing and when we fulfill our desires, we nurture through our acts. A desire fulfilled is never wanting, cannot be criticized or judged and is always, forever our own. A desire fulfilled is a magnet and attracts more and more to itself until we shine in our own light. A light that can never be dimmed or tarnished. We become alive because we are an expression of Life in its fullest—happiness, peace, beauty, joy, vitality!

Life (big 'L' Life) desires to evolve through us. When we sow from the heart. We reap Love.

The Dragon Dies

1 of 3

Can you name the dragon that feeds on your health and happiness?

Today was a bad day. It didn't start out that way, but a series of events—innocuous, small, some positive, some negative—started tripping me up, and the next thing I knew, I was on a spiral of dark feelings. I didn't want to be alone with myself and I didn't want to be with anyone—especially the one who loved me. I thought of calling a friend to see if she'd like to go to a show last minute, but decided she just might. Then I would be committed to either pretending I wasn't bleak or else inflicting upon her my useless whining about not being good enough!

Gawd! I grabbed my coat, shoved my phone and wallet in an inside pocket, and headed for the door. My son asked me where I was going and I called over my shoulder that I was going to a show.

"Alone?" he asked, surprised. "You can't go to a show alone! I'll go with you if you want."

"Uh uh." I was not fit company—even for myself—so I was going to plug into a big screen comedy and shove popcorn in my mouth.

I'd never actually been to a show by myself before. I was early even for the trailers and sat listening to Lou Rawles singing 'You're Gonna Miss My Lovin'.' I had a vague notion that life had been easier when that song came out. But that was no more true than the so-called "truths" my inner beast had been dishing me since mid-afternoon.

I couldn't grab hold of my usual assurances and concluded for the evening that it was so much easier to be negative than positive. That the chance of things turning out badly in spite of positive affirmations was so much more real than the chance of things turning out well. That, somehow, good outcomes would take more energy—more discipline—than bad. I knew I just had to ride out this night, and I believed a glass of wine followed by a good sleep would have me back to my sunny little self in the morning.

My phone battery was dead—natch—and after the film I called Athan from the pay phone. I was sure he would find my disappearance odd. He lived in the city and I was in the netherworld, halfway between the city and my home. Athan offered to meet me for coffee. Consistent with my mood, I halfheartedly tried to deflect his offer: "Are you sure you want to?" What a little girl!

I was glad he overlooked my lameness and said he was on his way. Times like these are not alien to me, as I am sure they are not for most from time to time. But I do know that when one is consciously reaching for a higher level of awareness and connection with spirit, the frequency might lessen but the intensity strengthens. Through my writing lately I have been dropping into a deeper place of remembering and integration of past events and their purpose and significance on a soul level. Clearing. Lightening. Ridding myself of what does not serve me.

I have always followed alternative and natural healing therapies, to support the physical plane of heredity, environment, emotion and spirit. In fact the piece I had been working on all morning had me thinking about the many layers we might use to interpret our state of balance in body, mind, and spirit. We are like filo pastries of information if we only knew how to read them. Herbology, naturopathy, and reflexology are some and of course all the Chinese medicines read the body like a finely charted map.

If the body doesn't efficiently process nutrients and eliminate all waste, stuff builds up, accumulates in corners and crevices, and becomes a breeding ground for toxins sapping the host body of nutrients and energy, until the depletion leads to weakened systems inviting biological predators.

When the body is in optimal health and not a fit environment, these organisms move through and are evacuated harmlessly. The body is efficient and intelligent, and is a natural healing organism. But if the body is dealing with various stresses and toxins, even natural therapies may lead to conditions getting worse before they get better. A battle rages for the supremacy of the strongest.

The soul also has such beasts, or "dragons," as I call them here. As we take in the information of life from the moment of birth, we ingest nutrients *and* toxins. We take in information and are left with emotional byproducts. We are pre-judgment at the outset, and by the time we may be questioning an external authority, often the parasite of negativity—in shame or unworthiness—has lodged safely in the dark of the mind and the soul. It feeds on negative emotions and grows stronger as it goes unchallenged. In fact, we set up circumstances to recreate the scene or script as it was laid out unconsciously, purely because it is with what we become familiar. Just as a beaten child will often end up in an abusive relationship, we are obscenely comforted by what we know—even if it hurts us. It is familiar and unchallenged, and somehow speaks to us in a voice that sounds true.

Negativity generally cautions us against failure, blame, embarrassment. It sounds so protective—a warning voice. It does this by warning you not to speak out because you might be wrong. Don't love because you might get hurt. Don't trust because you might be betrayed. Don't be different because you might look stupid. Negativity keeps you safe. It also keeps you prisoner—and worse, it will eventually bring to bear all the circumstances from which it kept you "safe."

Negativity also tells you to be like this person or that person because he or she is famous, successful, rich, beautiful. Of course, you can never be just like anyone else, so your inner negative voice will jeer at you for failing.

Once you begin to detox (through therapy or practice, psychologically or spiritually), you get lighter. The dragon is no longer so easily integrated into your personality. It becomes more obvious when it lashes out.

Then, as you gain strength in your own light of authenticity, the beast begins to writhe in its death throes. It even tricks you by staying really quiet until you begin to tip the scale into autonomy and authentic expression. With this comes confidence, esteem, and self-value. The dragon hates that. It cannot compete with true pleasure. It cannot thrive in love any more than cancer can in an alkaline host. Cancer needs an acidic body. The dragon needs fear and shame. Like a rat cornered, the beast fights to the end.

Unless we slay the dragon, it will go into remission and find some cranny of negativity to sustain it until it recovers. It will move us subtly into wrong decisions that, if we are not watchful and aware, will trap us in a cycle of disappointment or victimization. When we default to living unconsciously—reactive rather than proactive—the dragon rises up and the familiar voice will chide, "I told you so."

When I met Athan for hot chocolate after the movie, he said that my words on the phone had frightened him. I had said them "unconsciously" but, of course, it was the dragon speaking. They were words of fear and failure at the very time when I was being most successful in my heart's desires. It was the indication that the dragon was raising its ugly head in final assault and, if given the chance, would annihilate its very host. I realized even as I took myself off to a show alone I had purposely avoided the one who, with love, would hold the light for me. The dragon was in control.

So tonight I slay the dragon. I—who carry spiders outside—will slay the dragon. It's not what "nice" girls do, but I'm done with pain. I choose pleasure.

As I write, I reflect on the past week. Three days ago I said to my son, "You know, I am finally living the life I always dreamed of." It was that statement that sent the beast of negativity and unworthiness into stealth and final ambush today. Now I get it. In a way the dragon coming out so ferociously in daylight is good. It proves that I—and "all that I might be"—am alive and well, and the dragon is a myth of my own illusion.

A myth is a belief system that forms our life. Either this one will steal my joy, pleasure, success and health, or I will destroy it once and for all. My truths are daggers and my love is fire. The dragon dies!

The Dragon's Teeth

Do you feel the hot breath of self-doubt on your neck?

I am as passionate about the nature of business as I am about the nature of the body and spirit. For me, a card-carrying entrepreneur and risk taker, I devour books on business trends and strategies with equal pleasure as I do ancient spiritual teachings. I am as fascinated in how to develop a new market as I am in how to reveal the inner spark of creativity. Actually it's all the same to me.

Over the years my business has taken me into boardrooms with very powerful and wealthy corporate leaders. I have prepared investor memoranda, participated in corporate mergers, and facilitated strategic plans for integrating acquired divisions into a new corporate whole. I have witnessed a lot about business and learned even more about human nature. One thing in particular.

And what was that? Everyone, and I mean *everyone*, has a dragon breathing down his or her neck. I am using the example of business because we in the West have a notion that the rich and powerful are somehow also imminently confident and self-assured. That as long as someone is at the top of the food chain, there is no social higher authority. No fear. No dragon.

Problems, challenges and disappointments aren't dragons. In the dragon's teeth, we are firmly gripped in the fear of exposure of our unworthiness, inferiority, humiliation, shame, and guilt. None of us is any different. It is just the degree of our public display as we grapple with our own beasts of self-doubt.

Often people in the public eye—be it in the world of entertainment, business, or politics—actively seek out power, wealth, and influence as an armor against the dragon. We may even believe that the dragon is "out there"—the shareholders, the CEO, the constituents—the ones we have to assuage. The ones we have to stand up to with bravado. Never let them see the whites of your eyes, no fear, and no weakness. We furiously brick up a fortress of protection, with walls high and thick—fame, wealth, reputation, status, authority, even deception and coercion—only to find that, oops, the dragon is inside.

We may not know it until we are about to go on stage, take the podium or meet the new chairman. The dragon snorts and the fire burns in our solar plexus. Our place of will and self-esteem. The fire spreads down into our gut and reaches up to set our heart drumming and sear our mind. In that instant—before we repeat the affirmation, take the pill, shoot the Stolis, or otherwise submerge the dragon, we are caught aware of our own incompleteness. But…so what?

Dragons wreak havoc. When they are awakened and come out of the cave, snorting fire and swinging their spiked tails, destruction and incineration decimates the landscape. Just look at the recent banking debacle. Who hasn't been affected by that melee of greed and avarice? Dragons on a feeding frenzy. But how can dragons be on the inside and the outside at the same time?

Dragons start out small. A little piece of misinformation in the psyche. Something your mother said when she was tired that made you feel unloved. Something your classmates said to you because you were different and you felt humiliation. Your teacher made an example of you in front of the class and you felt angry and powerless at the same time. Your father shouted and hit your brother, and you knew fear. Someone you trusted touched you when you said no, and you felt shame. Emotions. Potent electrical and chemical currents surge through the body, lodging in the cells, and recording in the brain. And, like tiny magnets of energy, they attract similar emotions. The event is over. Come and gone. Maybe not even witnessed by another. But its effect remains and gathers strength.

Shame, fear, humiliation, anger, powerlessness, unworthiness. Tiny dragons. They wake you up in the night. They begin to feed on your happiness. When 'feel good' things happen, they eat them up and ask for more. More food, more things, more attention, more control. Even dragons hush when they feed. So we keep feeding them, trying to keep them quiet and under control. But in actuality they are just getting stronger and bigger until they burst the seams of your psyche and create a life outside of you as well. Dragons poke you in your "wants" and drive you forward. "A bigger house and I'll be quiet." "A higher position and I'll be quiet." "A faster car and I'll be quiet." "A younger lover and I'll be quiet."

But of course, dragons are too clever to let you see them first thing in the morning, dirty scales, smoking nostrils and all. No, material avarice is not the only language of dragons. Dragons outside of you act through your wife, your boss, your children, the media. Dragons roar equally loudly through the morally superior, the pious, the self-deprecating, the intellectual. Here is the secret to reveal the dragon: Anyone whom you feel the need to please is the voice of the dragon.

The caveat is that the voice of the dragon is not the actual inner dragon. It is the magnification of the dragon. Its projection on the big screen. The real dragon is still safe, growing teeth and scales deep inside your soul. It will remain safe while you are distracted with slaying the dragon of your outer world. While it grows unimpeded within, it will never, ever, be vanquished. Ultimately the dragon will lead you to the fullest expression of the seed that spawned it: humiliation, loss of love, shame, ruin. Just like the parasite it is, the dragon will feed on the host until the death of both.

To lead an epic life—worthy of heroes and heroines—is to slay the dragon forever. Once this predator of happiness, self-worth, pleasure, accomplishment, and creativity is gone and no longer a fearsome ruler, you can enjoy all that is truly meaningful to you.

Your light—the elements that make you uniquely you—will be revered and loved. The truth that you speak and the love that you share will be all you need to attract a life you truly desire. A life that allows you to share your wisdom, creativity, and knowledge—your joy and happiness. A life that may be expressed in simplicity or in grandeur. You may be a monk or a king. A sculptor or a mother. A CEO or a courier. You might build a school in Malawi or a corporation in Silicon Valley. But you will do it from the heart.

For it is the heart that is imprisoned in the cave of the beast. A heart pulsing in full expression of love, light, and creativity dissolves the dragon. The damsel in distress is the frail self—our own innocent heart—beautiful, sensitive, loveable. The spark of Life itself; the promise of all that we can be.

How do I know this? Because yesterday the beast showed its face to me. In outer appearances I have it all. A beautiful home, my own business, regard amongst my peers, a loving relationship, two amazing, creative sons, and a deep, spiritual life. But for all that I have accomplished and all that I enjoy, my default when I was tired or stressed was to anxiety, fear and self-doubt. There are no actual facts supporting that. So where was it coming from? And what is the gain in maintaining it? There is no conscious gain. The dragon lives on unconscious acts. As soon as you begin to make conscious choices, the dragon is threatened. As light floods in, the dragon fades.

Once the dragon is released from the heart we truly do live happily ever after.

In the Eye of the Dragon
3 of 3

How to reclaim your heart.

The dragon must die but to vanquish it, it must be lured from the cave into the light. All this drama of heroes, damsels, dragons, heart, and self, courage, and fear is the stuff of our daily life on Earth. Applying the archetypes only facilitates in understanding the active energy of these forces as they motivate or limit us from within, and as they attract external circumstances and relationships to perpetuate and feed the momentum of self-deception—the dragon.

We can all relate to the interplay of these forces in our personal evolution. Whether we are born onto the sunny coast of California or the broken streets of Beirut, our personal story unfolds and undulates in response to internal and external influences. We are reactive or proactive, and as we strengthen within, the forces without are mitigated. So, the dragon we slay is the force of limitation on our personal evolution. And what exactly are we limiting? What is our personal evolution? And how does that impact on the world we live in?

My own learning began with a quest. It was a quest to avoid pain and suffering and to live without fear. I wasn't even thinking in terms of happiness, creativity, and personal fulfillment in those days. I just wanted to come up to a baseline. The actual circumstances are immaterial, as the relevance lies only in the cumulative affect on my psyche and the ultimate claim for release. I did not want to be another statistic in my family of depression or suicide, or penitent to a moralistic belief. And I certainly didn't want that kind of influence on the children I was bringing into this turbulent world.

Consequently, I have been a passionate student of all ways of healing. Spiritual, energetic, nutritional, physical, and intellectual. My own search for answers and the subsequent trip of healing, through tragedy, betrayal and disillusionment into lightness, comprehension, and reverence is the foundation of my vision of LightBeam and all aspects of my life work and contribution.

I was a seeker for many years until I began to study the ancient teachings of Patañjali and the *Bhagavad Gita*. They were very obscure to me and my Western mind had great trouble in interpreting the texts. However, my most beloved teacher, Gita, assured us that if we followed the lessons in our own time and did not rush, understanding would come. She also made a very portentous observation. She said, "Just be aware that when you study sacred texts, your life will draw in the circumstances to illustrate the lessons."

That has been absolutely true and the way—though rough—has been resplendent with growing awareness for the subtle and sublime Life force that imbues every creature, rock, and star in this wide universe. The more my understanding expanded, the less division there was in this way or that way. This doctrine or that dogma. Life began to express itself in a sense of extreme individuality and uniqueness—no two snowflakes alike—and at the same time, the amazing unity and interdependence of all living systems—molecules or galaxies. I found confidence in my own voice humming my tune and delighted in the collective voice of all who wished to sing along with me.

I began to use the mantra, "I create the world I want to live in and it is populated with people I love and respect." This is indeed unfolding and that world is pretty small, but it is vibrant and full of color, laughter, friendship, creativity, and accomplishment. I've lost my way a few times, but as I described in *The Dragon Dies* and *The Dragon's Teeth*, those missteps become more evident and corrected to bring me back to peace and confidence.

In this world of instant everything, we tend to believe that we can read a book, take a course, visualize or will a state into existence. We can most certainly be transformed by any of these. But the act of personal evolution is a lifetime of awakenings and glimpses of all that we can be. We then experience this awareness on all levels—body, mind, emotion, soul, and then anchor it into our consciousness. It is in this deep integration of healing on all levels that we truly affect the world we live in.

Our Life's purpose is to fulfill our own soul destiny. In this way we are truly co-contributors of Life's evolution. We are the very cells of Life's creative body. As we take in information, process it and express it in our daily lives, we construct a world of deeper understanding, interdependence, and interconnectedness. We are manifestations of the nature and the natural order of Life as surely as the trees and galaxies. The difference—as far as we know at this moment in time—is that we are conscious and can exert our conscious will over our actions and processes.

While the natural world expands and evolves, ebbs and flows, rises and falls on an ever-undulating course, we conscious beings affect the expanding consciousness of the world. The collective emotion: The evolution of happiness over despair, peace over war, care over abuse. It is not difficult to see that the world is in chaos. There is starvation, torture, war, decimation, pollution, greed, anguish, suffering. The dragon of our collective unconsciousness is wreaking havoc. It's breathing poison into our water, ash into our air, starving our children, and singeing all our necks with the terror of uncertainty.

There is so much that people are doing to shift all this. Global prayer vigils, exhortations to God, blogs by the trillions, political and social activism. But all this activity—passive and aggressive—misses the whole point. The dragon grows in strength and power, not because we are focusing our attention and giving it energy, but because the dragon in our outer world is only the distraction for the dragon within us. The little dragon that would be safe stays safe because we ignore it to focus on the wrongs of the outer world. As long as we stay focused on the evil, greedy conniving bastards of the—name it—banks, pharmaceutical companies, governments, fishing fleets, fur traders, deforesters, munitions producers, we are neatly caught in the net of self-delusion.

In turn, the collective consciousness is displayed in the world around us. I don't know anyone who wouldn't like to live somewhere beautiful—a beach, the mountains, surrounded by love, and enjoying creative peace and serenity. We look at the world and wonder who made this mess? Clearly it is not our choice but here it is. The dragon of war, pollution, genocide, disease and poverty feeds on our collective delusion, our collective *collusion* to blame others, and it gets fat on our collective doubt and uncertainty.

Inside the acorn is the entire imprint for the oak. Given the basic conditions of clean water, fresh air, and nutrients from the earth, the oak will flourish. Within the acorn lies all the oak can potentially achieve. Drought and lightning may alter its shape, but within it remains all it might be. Likewise, within us is all that we might be. If we are to be a musician, we will hear or see music and be drawn to its expression. Being human, our expression of our complete potential is not only affected by environment conditions, but also by conditions of consciousness.

As Life's expression of conscious evolution, we are given the added ingredient of will. We don't automatically evolve to the highest expression of our personal Self. We must *choose* to fulfill our highest potential. Enter the dragon. The dragon is all that is not true about us.

Before it outgrows the boundaries of our soul and leaps into the arena of the collective conscious, it feeds and gets powerful on self-doubt. And how are we relieved of self-doubt? By calling it out and looking it right in the eye. When we have the courage to face our fears—and sometimes we need help—we will see that they are not based on fact, but on false beliefs, which have grown out of control and choke our potential for a creative, healthy, and prosperous life.

Peace and love are our natural state of being; they are the stuff of our heart's desire. They are always there, within. Sometimes deep in the cave, behind the fearsome dragon. Call the dragon out; see the lies in its eyes of what you believe about yourself that is not true. Then raise the daggers of all your talents, gifts, and goodness of who you really are and slay it, now. Each time the voice within you breathes the fire of doubt, shame, guilt, unworthiness; face it down with another truth. Keep doing it until the dragon is silent. Then, puff! The dragon becomes magical and when it rises (and it will), it will be your ally—your reminder of who you really are!

When your heart is finally free from bondage, peace and love will fill you to overflowing and then the pulse of the world will change at last.

The Wrong End of the Telescope

How a simple reversal of perspective will give you the life you desire.

But first I have to share a word with you that is so significant to our health and happiness, that it is the only key to our personal joy and to the flourishing of the earth and the universe she rests in. So mystical is this word that it frightens us and wakes us in the night, and causes war among brothers. So magical is this word that when we say it with understanding, we are liberated from all fears—forever. This word represents a gift of creation so powerful that it rivals the miracle of our birth. And that word is Death.

Birth and death are the parenthesis of our life on earth. And what transpires within those brackets (into the world and out) is our Life. Life can be short and meaningful as a Japanese Haiku or fraught with the drama of a Greek Tragedy in multiple acts. Because we fear death more than revere it, we live our lives as if we might somehow avoid it altogether. Illness, accident or old age—the vehicles of death always seem to take us by surprise—as some sort of mistake in judgment or wrong turn. If only she hadn't smoked, if only he had made a full stop, if only she had taken her vitamins. Death is, at once, the ultimate certainty and the ultimate mystery.

The fact is that as surely as you are reading this you were born and as surely as you were born you will die—sooner or later. The journey to that final door marked Death is your true Life purpose. Forget worrying about what your Life purpose might be—you are living it even as you search. Forget, "When I have my own apartment, car, million, private plane, I'll be okay." Forget, "When my children are grown, when I have enough money, when I retire, I will paint, write, garden." Replace the word "then" with the word "now." Take a deep breath. Exhale out loud and listen to that exhalation. That is you breathing. That is you alive.

When the stork dropped you, he dropped you with a sack of goodies. Rudimentary supplies to get you started. Girl, boy, black, white, yellow. The soul of a poet; the mind of a mathematician. It is an intriguing mix of potentialities. Your mother's eyes, your father's walk—immediate stuff. But you also have a blend of their blend. Going back just two hundred years or ten generations to 1811, 1,024 people had to have intimate encounters for you to be here now. If you multiply 1,024 by the number of genes—both latent and dominant—then you have a staggering complexity of possibilities in your makeup. To follow your line back to the beginning of time, well, you have to think in terms of stars and galaxies to grasp the limitless possibilities.

But that's not all! Your baby sack got dropped into a garden, concrete jungle or warzone. And your family either thought it was a good thing or not a good thing that you were born, and they cried, smiled or cussed. Now imagine rising up at lightening speed above your crib until you are amongst the stars looking down and seeing all the living beings on the planet—nearly seven billion—and how their thoughts and actions tilt the world mood and outcome like a teeter totter between Nirvana and Armageddon. Now you have a minute sense of the potential influence of heredity and environment.

But heredity and environment are only what is in your bag. It is not YOU. Your body is the physical draping around the spark of Life that is your pure potential. The oak within the acorn. Your brain is the recorder and processor of information, and your conscious mind—awareness—is your connection with all of Life. Consciousness is not a connection in the sense of a thread or umbilical attachment, but rather like cupping your hands under the water of the ocean. Your body is the physical envelope if you will, but the whole of the creative Life force fills you and surrounds you and ebbs and flows. It is in you and all around you at the same time. It is in you and every other person, mineral, plant or planet.

Your life began with a choice and is continually micro-directed by every subsequent choice. The first choice was not the obvious one of "him" and "her;" otherwise all siblings would be identical. The first choice that defined you was *this* sperm and *tha*t egg. Now depending on how quickly you individuated and made your own conscious choices, the sooner you took charge and shaped life according to your deepest desires. You might have been allowed to pair orange and purple as matched socks when you were little or your mother still picked out your shirt and tie for your first job interview. Whichever the case, your heart's desires were either expressed or repressed.

If you have had a difficult life or are enduring a patch you don't like, you might complain that you didn't choose to be born. No one in his or her "right mind" would choose to be born to an abusive parent or some other unfortunate circumstance, but your mind didn't do the choosing. In its desire for evolution and creation, Life chose to be born through you. The difference between an animal or rock and a human being is that the creative Life force called Nature continues to make the choices. You, the human being, on the other hand, are aware that you are conscious and so have the will to move with and express Nature through your choices and actions, or override and repress Nature.

So what does that have to do with your mixed bag of heredity and environment, and your eventual death? And what does this all have to do with health and happiness? Well, only this: *Everything*. It really may seem with all the infinite possibilities in your makeup, that finding a thread and being solely responsible for creating your life tapestry might seem too complex. There are just too many outside influences and responsibilities, and on top of all that the world is in chaos. What can you really do? You can't change the world chaos any more than you can hold back the tides or stop the earth in its orbit. And if you believed you could—how would you manage those choices?

It is actually sublimely simple: What do you desire? The energy of Life starts within and works outward. The oak is already in the acorn. When the acorn falls on the forest floor and takes root, all its energetic focus is on being what it is. An oak. It reaches into the soil for nourishment and water. It reaches skyward toward the life giving light of the sun. It takes up its space in the earth, in the forest, in the air necessary to fulfill its wholeness. Lichen on the rock beside it, or a tiny plant of wintergreen sprouting waxy leaves and red berries fulfill the "self" same mandate of all that it can be. There is no competition or desire to be other than it is. Each has its own space and influence on the whole of its environment.

As human beings, our "oak" of Self—actualized—is within us and requires our conscious participation; our free will. We choose how we root into the soil of our physical environment. How we create and share in the abundance that surrounds us in our community, and ultimately how we influence the world in which we live. As humans we are born with basic propensities within an environmental context. Infinite possibilities. How we play it out is entirely up to us. Pleasure or pain; joy or sorrow. Only in following the inner wisdom of our heart's true desires will we know how to ride either/or on the buoyancy of a good life well lived!

When we lay our head down on the pillow for the last time, not even then knowing exactly when we will exhale for the last time, what will be running through our mind as important? The thing is: As we look at the infinite odds that conspired in our unique blend of genes to become us—the microcosm—and then look up to the night sky and imagine those trillions of stars and galaxies—the macrocosm—we glimpse the actual significance of our personal life role in the scheme of the whole of the universe for all time. The only thing that matters is what our life meant to *us*.

Do you love? Are you loved? Are you fulfilled? If your name is called tomorrow, are you ready to let go? Up until that last breath will you have been all that you might be—and know the blessing that you are?

When do you Give Up on Yourself?

How do you measure success?

Yesterday I had tea with a friend who had recently had the occasion to chat with Kevin O'Leary of *Dragons' Den* and *Shark Tank*. These are the gems of advice he offered her:

If you can't articulate what your business is about in ninety seconds, no one will invest in you

Successful people have to be prepared to spend eighteen-hour days for some duration

Spend your time not your money, and finally…

Know when to get out

My friend queried me on the last point. "How do you know when it's time to call it a day, or when you've spent enough money—when do you decide your great idea just isn't going to fly?" Of course, I had to confess that I was probably the wrong person to ask about that. I still believe in my business vision that I first diagrammed on a flip chart in my (then) web designer's boardroom. That was five years ago. It showed overlapping circles (a vesica piscis) depicting autonomous businesses collaborating to the greater good of all. The foundation of that business exists. It is the LightBeam wheel of websites. It echoes a little—okay, it echoes a lot—because it's waiting for the people to populate it. It's innovative and a slightly different way to use the Internet—and the

Internet itself is an ever-changing mystery to many. More on this later.

After my afternoon meeting, I was off to meet another friend for dinner. As we walked around the block arm in arm over icy patches she asked about my sons—were they off on their European tour with the band this summer? Hmm…she was a little out of date. I had to explain that those plans had been side-railed because, one afternoon the savvy and beautiful promoter and manager known as "Ms. A" had taken a powder on the way to a meeting to discuss the imminent tour date. "Oh," replied my friend, raising an eyebrow. "Do you think they should do something else?" My immediate response was no! These young men are good musicians and they have a unique sound. When I envision them, I see them pressing against the membrane, just about to break through.

Now, before you conclude that an innovator mother with unrealistic goals has spawned sons with unrealistic rock star aspirations, let me rush in and say this: I'm not stupid, and just like everyone else I get dragged down by "reality." So on the way home, I was blue. Doubt was hanging about me like a pall. Fear comes rushing in because I am the sole supporter of my family and that scares me at times. And then can self-recrimination be far behind when I think that most parents would have "made" their sons be realistic and get jobs—or even go back to school?

So I stopped on my way out of town as I passed Athan's door for a quick pick-me-up hug. "Everything is going to be okay—isn't it?" I muffled into his shoulder. Athan held me at arm's length, looked deep into my eyes and said, "Of course! And even if it isn't okay—it will be 'okay'." Now it might seem that he was patronizing me and sending me off with a "Now, now, there, there," but the effect of his words ripped away the mask of "reality" and I was once again looking at the meaning of life.

These reality shows are a true barometer of our times. They are a reflection of the distortion that we call life. In a way I wonder if they are the backlash of the times—most recent—when schools, parents, and sports leagues all decided that competition was somehow unfair. That failure discriminated unfairly, that success must be equilateral or shared. These shows are based on humiliation of the many and the exploitation of the one. The "one" has to fit a very specific criteria and the "win" is not based on excellence but in compliance.

It is the archetype of the worst father who disinherits his child if he does not comply with the family way of excellence. It is social coercion at its most nihilistic. Fit the mold—or live alone in mortification!

I'd be bleeding all over the stage if I presented my innovative business model on an aforementioned TV show. My heart would be pounding to the clock ticking down ninety seconds. BEEEEEEP! Time's up: You're fired! Oh—wrong show. My business is about holistic living; body, mind, and spirit. These dudes are so out of harmony with the natural and pleasurable aspects of life, that they probably wouldn't get my concept if I drew a thirty-second Venn diagram. It's helpful to be able to sum up your business in a few phrases, but Life as reflected in our business is more than a few sound bites. And here's why:

Our real business is not what we do for a living. It's not what we exchange for money. Our real business is our own Life—in all its complexity, troubles, and pleasures. Our family, our work, our engagement with the world we live in is the playing field where we discover who we are. Our talents, our strengths, our weaknesses, our desires and our dreams, and most of all: Our contribution to the evolution of this world. We are not here just to put in time as people—a general population—but as contributing energy to the direction the world will take—"good" or "bad."

When we focus too much on success for success's sake we rush to results before we look to effects. When I was in the construction industry, it became evident through the very nature of building how the culture of a region or country viewed their responsibility or accountability to the future. Our business was architectural entranceways, including revolving or security doors for banks, hotels and condominiums.

They were grand—you never get a second chance to make a first impression—in polished bronze or mirror stainless steel. Here's a thumbnail of different perspectives, in very general terms:

The west coast—Canada and US—had a "disposable" perspective. They would not invest in high quality, because the architectural landscape (aka "trends") changed so often that buildings would go up with a lifespan already in mind. The emphasis was on glamor, flash, and price. Some of these buildings are notorious; high profile with paper-thin walls. Big hype for quick sales—high class, low fees—only to find in the fullness of time that the shortcuts taken in construction are in short order catching up with the owners in gargantuan fee increases.

New York, Chicago, Toronto, London; cities of banks and investors, chose elegant and stately designs, and considered the front entrance as a cost percentage of the overall value of the property. The architect has a greater influence on quality products and consistency of durability than on the coasts, where design built is more initial profit oriented.

Interestingly, in Asia companies we dealt with spoke in terms of generations, of legacy. One company was over five hundred years old! Their responsibility to the future was a guiding principle. Every aspect of a building was efficient, beautiful and resilient—constructed to last and be a tribute to those who created it.

When we create our own life, on what do we place our values? What is our unique contribution? What is our legacy? How are we accountable and how do we leave the world a better place?

My sons are musicians—that is what they are. So many "advise" them and me that you really can't make it in the music business—it's too long a shot to be a star. Maybe, some suggest, they should go on *Canadian Idol*. Now one thing is for sure: You can't make it in the music business if you don't make music your business. Since the disappearance of Ms. A, the band has discovered that they really don't need her after all. They have developed a business plan, designed the logo, nearly finished the MySpace page, written an album's worth of original music, are mastering a demo tape, created a "merch" list—the T-shirts are already in and selling like mad. In fact my youngest can already claim, "Been there, done that, got the tat!" The thing is, the world of music has become so sophisticated, that an artist is expected to instantly have the same complete package that in the past would have been provided by the record label.

In my mind, this change is for the better. My sons have strengthened in experience and competence in ways that a "real" education couldn't begin to offer. Secondly, they have by necessity and disappointment become knowledgeable and savvy, developing traits that will stand them in strength in a business that is notorious for manipulation and exploitation. They have learned the value of creativity—in their case, music—to heal from loss and grief. They have, as brothers, come to ways of collaborating to use the best of each one's talents—musically and business wise. They work with the two other group members with a maturity, discipline, and diplomacy that would do well in the largest corporation.

So, as a mother, I am incredibly proud of their work and their accomplishments. The fact that they haven't "made it" yet is almost inconsequential to the point of who they have become, and the stability they have gained will help them ride the crazy world of excess everyone loves to hate in the entertainment world.

As for me, my lack of "success" as reflected in my present bank account and credit rating doesn't begin to disclose my own path of fine-tuning, learning, growing, resilience, and courage. Yes, I can say that about myself—even though I was taught not to take too much credit for myself. These past five years included the illness and death of my husband, embezzlement and fraud within the web design company I trusted, the erosion of all my capital, and realization that the world was not quite ready for what I offered.

My belief in the LightBeam vision kept me sane through the devastating grief of losing my husband, business partner and the father of our still-young boys. In desperation I began to take courses on websites and Internet marketing—just so my nefarious web designers couldn't dupe me. What started out as the fury and fear of walking away from tens of thousands of dollars in web design that never worked turned into my own competence and understanding of open source software platforms; outsourcing; Internet marketing and the nature of the Internet in general. Collaboration in the highest terms—by strangers for strangers! For free! Awesome!

Dreams are the vision of all that is possible. Without dreams there are no realities. Dreams hold us steady while all that is in the chaos of creation sorts itself. Like an epic voyage, my adventure in fulfilling my vision has led me on a circuitous route to the center of my own being. Opportunities that I dreamed of years ago are now coming forth because all the elements for real success had to evolve until the timing was right. And that time is now.

Eighteen-hour days? Oh yeah. But when you are doing what you love, they are not eighteen-hour days of slugging or slavery during which you work for someone else's dream. They are inspired and inspiring days that often run into nights. Dreams can wake you up to the most amazing solutions to a nagging problem. Often a solution that defies logic—and often a solution that you could never get from someone else's vision.

Spend your time, not your money. I had to nearly exhaust my capital before I figured out that self-proclaimed experts were rarely that. Especially in the Internet world, which changes in a heartbeat. Being of a trusting nature and deferring to an authority leads an entrepreneur on the downhill spiral of, "An innocent and his money are soon parted!" Take the time to learn what your business connects to and relies on so that you too can spot a scammer.

How do I measure success? I am happy, confident in my own abilities, and have something to make the world a brighter place. I have gained knowledge and wisdom. When will I be rich? I am enriched in self-love and self-respect—can I ever be poor? Even if it's not okay (by whatever standards I might set), it will be "okay"—it will be more of my own beautiful life unfolding! When do you give up on yourself? Never!

In Pursuit of Happiness

Do you have time to be happy?

It was about 4:00AM when I woke this morning. I lay in bed, inviting sleep back and feeling the nameless dreads lurking in the corner of my mind. What should I do about selling the house? What should I do about the car that caught fire today? Why am I clenching my teeth? I resorted to my trusted remedy—a few drops of lavender oil on my pillow—and twirled my Nano to a meditation. Finally, away I drifted.

Unfortunately I "drifted" right into a very nasty dream.

I was in a large car dealership reporting to the sales manager. I was their outside agent and doing very well at bringing in corporate clients. The owner—a sleazy, menacing man—came over and said, never mind the manager, I was to deal directly with him—at which point he began to molest me. I raised myself to full height and told him to drop dead—didn't he know who I was? But that didn't stop him and he began to overpower me. I started screaming for everybody to see this creep and what he was doing.

But no one paid any attention. Even a group of young women employees glanced at me and then looked away. I realized I was completely vulnerable in this cavernous space that he owned, where he had paralyzed everyone in the place into fear of retribution. Somehow I broke free of his deplorable clutches and made a dash outside to my car. It was now after dark. The parking lot was huge and offered no safety or hope of intervention. My car was the only escape. But no! I discovered I had left my keys on the sales manager's desk. Facing my fear, I ran back in. The creep let me in and out again, and I knew he was sure of his victory, and was playing with my fear.

I made it to my car but was unable to lock the doors before he jumped into the passenger seat. I careened out of the parking lot, keeping the car off balance. Finding a busy street, I jammed the car into park, leapt out the door and into a large and crowded store. In true, dreamlike fashion, it was a Halloween costume store, full of women lined up to buy fluorescent wigs and such. The creep followed me in, now in a rage, and began attacking and punching in earnest. I screamed again to draw attention, but all the women looked and then looked away. I shouted at one woman that I couldn't let this man frighten me and make me fearful in the future. She replied that, judging from the rage in his face, I had angered someone who would now never let me alone. I was frantic with fear! He knew where I lived!

I ran back to my car and got away—only to have him shoot out the tire. In a flash, I pictured a life plagued by this stalker who meant me harm—but worse, meant to torment me with fear of harm. In that second, I realized I would rather die than live in fear. I jumped out of the car and opened my coat so he could shoot me in the heart. And then I woke up.

Usually other people's dreams aren't very interesting if you're not a Jungian, but I recount this as I think, in a way, it is everyone's dream. And I know it was spawned by the conversation my mate and I had that afternoon. I was waiting for a friend whom I had driven to a hospital appointment. Athan had come to wile away the time with me, and we found a quiet place at the back of the hospital property. We sat on a stone wall with our legs dangling over the edge, and looked down over a formidable drop into the valley below. High up in one of the trees, a raccoon lay curled and sleeping. Above, a hawk swung in lazy swoops. A creek was beginning to emerge from its snowy banks. It was peaceful and warm in the spring-like sun.

We were talking about this and that—how my car caught fire and all. A dear friend of mine, aged ninety, had died that week and I shared my sadness for a long life lived in duty and not joy. This gave rise to the question of why humans are conscious. It seems rather cruel to have a physical body and a physical life only to know that we are destined to die. What is the point in that? Neanderthals weren't troubled by that concept presumably. So why this development of knowing? Does it give us meaning or does it give us fear? Or both?

Being a student of the spiritual path—in many forms—I opined on co-creating, evolution, and a greater meaning. But Athan, in his usual forthright fashion, asked me what difference a hereafter really made to this life now. Before I got too huffy, he went on to say that so many near death experiences included the white light tunnel and the feeling of immense love. Tap into a hundred-year-old coffin, and once you blow the dust away and pick up the skull, you can ask it, "How's the white light working for you now?"

I started to laugh because that is absolutely true. We have constructed our whole world out of the need to have meaning beyond this life. But this is the only life we have going at this precise moment. We have created a society and a culture around things—structures, objects, laws, and businesses that keep us safe and alive and busy thinking about keeping ourselves safe and alive. And then there's all the acquired wisdom, both new age and ancient, assuaging our worried souls that there is a reason for suffering and things will be clear "on the other side." But what about the here and now?

Athan and I sat in the sun, overlooking a picturesque creek and valley. Except for a few cans, bottles, and blue plastic buckets, it could have been hundreds of years ago. Our back was turned to the century stone house behind us. Beyond that were rings of construction fencing, leading up to the huge complex of the hospital growing in our very presence. Beyond that was the fifth largest city in North America: Toronto. The biggest buildings were churches, hospitals, banks, insurance companies. Save your soul! Save your life! Save your money! Save your house! Identical malls sprawled within blocks of each other, clamoring for consumer attention. To feel this—buy that! To be this—wear that! Belong or be outcast.

We are unequivocally living in a construct of fear. And where is the happiness in that? Where is the creativity as we ding like pinballs around the obstacle course of our lives? We distract ourselves with meaningless diversions.

If we have heartfelt pleasures we often hurry through them to get back to "all we have to do." Or worse, we save our pleasures for when we have time—which we rarely do. We fall in love and then wrench the tender shoots from the earth to see if it is growing like everybody says it should. We have or acquire a child and then wear it as an accessory. Will it walk before one, talk before two and read from a book at three? If the child rebels, can we give it Ritalin? We create a song, a poem or a dance and then offer it up to be crushed and ridiculed by millions nationwide.

We have completely given over our heart's desires to a collective unconscious. We have chosen to stay distracted by often nameless fears from the very thing our consciousness provides us, and that is the awareness of our own eventual death.

Why should we be preoccupied by death? We shouldn't be preoccupied or fearful of death—only aware of its inevitability. It is this awareness that defines what is actually precious and of value to us otherwise we die without ever really living. No wonder we fear death. It is the final confrontation that we have spent our lives guided by anything but the truth. And what is the truth? Whatever makes you happy. Truly heart light happy.

Happiness comes from the well of the heart and the heart is fed from the font of creation. True happiness comes from acts of love. The love of science, nature, commerce or humanity. As long as we are true to ourselves, we can never be wrong. And then we can die fearless and at peace, in the white light of our own creative accomplishments. Our legacy to a world that no longer holds us.

Does God Have a Sense of Humor?

2 of 3

You bet. We call it irony!

Remember the bad dream I mentioned in my last story? Well the next day, I got to live it! Isn't that ironic?

I figured the car fire was, in a way, a good thing. I'd call the insurance company; they would write off the car as being too old to warrant repair and I'd get something more reliable. As it happened, the deductible was way more than the repair and the repair was way more than I could afford right now. So just when I thought I was catching a break, I was actually getting another slap. What was that about? Well, one thing—it wasn't about the smack—it was about the punch to the solar plexus that was about to knock the wind out of me!

When I called my insurance broker of nearly thirty years, I was feeling the full force of my financial bind. Not being able to sell my house over the past two years has been a test of trust that the universe would unfold and somehow I wouldn't get pinched in the creases. The best advisors, well-meaning friends and I, myself, agreed that I gotta go. But, I'm sure I'm not sharing anything of great incidence when I say that this economic meltdown has dominoes falling the size of Stonehenge! The fallout has affected us all.

My broker said in his Eeyore drawl, "You can lead a horse to water, but you can't make them drink."

"Huh?" I responded.

"Marilyn, I told you years ago about XYZ who would give you a huge line of credit based on your equity, and you didn't do anything about it."

"Well, tell me again—I'm listening now!" I certainly didn't recall our previous conversation, but it may have occurred just when my husband died and I was not making major banking decisions at that time...or actually thinking at all.

"I'll have the agent call you and we'll have this in place in no time."

Wow! The clouds parted, the sun shone, and my phone rang. It was the other agent. He reminded me we had spoken some time ago and I didn't get back to him. Mmm...same "excuse."

"Let me take down a little information and we'll have this done today!"

He took all the info and then, as he was finishing up said, "Of course you have to have a good credit rating..."

"Actually," I said, "You're going to have to pull a few rabbits from the hat on that one. I have a lousy credit rating because I have been in survival priority mode and late on repayments many times."

How could I explain that sometimes weeks passed when I simply didn't pick up mail, let alone open it? There is no entry on the form that says when the polestar of your whole life is extinguished your universe shifts, and things take more than a little time to regain a cogent orbit. Anyway, he was as efficient in delivering the bad news as he was in promising the good. The irony? If all my affairs were in order and I didn't actually need the help, I would have gotten the green light!

My "score" was off by a few points and he said, "I wish you'd called me six months ago."

"Yeah, well, I wish my husband didn't die. But there you are. Stuff happens." I couldn't resist reinforcing the obvious.

That was a quick rollercoaster ride between hope and despair.

Despair? Why despair? My worst-case scenario is better than a lot of people's best-case dreams. And what does this have to do with happiness, fear, irony and a bad dream? Just this:

The path of enlightenment or spiritual mastery is the path of freedom—to the simple values of love, peace, and happiness. Love is the energy of all of creation. It is all there really is. Peace is the state of calm no matter what circumstances you experience. And happiness is the tiny pulse of joy that is sometimes glimpsed for short moments, but mostly suffocated in all the stuff we think is more important.

I asked for this mastery and so I am learning it. Some years ago, just before George died, I was studying the yoga sutras (sacred texts) and my beloved teacher told us, "Remember, when you begin this study, your life will offer the experiences to illustrate these lessons." My growing up was full of many sudden tragic losses and separations. My grandfather, my adored aunt, and dear big brother all committed suicide. My mother was hospitalized when I was three and she didn't come home until I was nine—the same year my aunt died. So when George got sick, I was in abject terror.

I think I tried to bargain with God to exchange a million little fears for the one big one. How could I possibly lose the man who once said to me in a time of self-doubt: "I know you better than you know yourself and I will love you until you love yourself"? How could this mountain of protection crumble? But he did and my mastery over fear and the first steps of enlightenment (lightening up) began. So in the grander scheme of things—how does a credit rating really rate?

My agent seemed to sense my dismay as an invitation to give his opinion of all I should have done that I didn't do. He finished off by saying, "You'll just have to sell the house and get a condo, pay your bills on time and learn to live a different lifestyle!" I wondered what lifestyle he was referring to. It sounded like the one where I drink champagne in my spare time when I'm not buying shoes. It certainly wasn't the one that I'm familiar with. However, the truth notwithstanding, I could feel all the joy in my many accomplishments draining from my soul like blood from a wound. The irony that everyone seems to miss is that it was the banks' abuse of credit that caused this collapse in the first place. And here nearly two years later we're still feeling the seismic after-effects.

The dramas we live and play out are never really what they appear to be about. Instead they are about unveiling our weaknesses and polishing our strengths. The US Army says, "Be all you can be," and to get there they put a cadet through rigorous training to expose any negatives that might come out at the wrong moment; endangering the soldier and all who depend on him.

So yesterday I spent the day doing the things that I could do to solve my immediate problem. To do that I had to ask for help—which is to admit that I can't do this by myself. It is a lesson in humility. There is a solution and it may be different from what I expect. A lesson in detachment.

This morning I woke up thinking about this writing and, before I knew it, my throat began to close up. My heart was pounding and I was racing toward a full-blown panic attack! What was this about? I did three things before I was calm enough to see what these past days were for. First, I got hold of the runaway mustang of my mind racing to join the stampede of thoughts of doom. Second, I took some Dr. Bach's Rescue Remedy (where would a new mother or bride on her wedding day be without it?) and third, I got down on my yoga mat and began my series of sun salutations. I took a moment longer and did some reflexology on my hands and feet to release the stress in my neck. And then I began to bring some objectivity to this drama. Again, it's never about what it seems to be about. It's inevitably about our own mastery, and to get caught in the drama is to miss the whole opportunity.

Yesterday I found myself recounting the family suicides to a friend who didn't know. I wondered why I did that. Then I realized it was this month that my brother died. Our souls recall anniversaries so that we can heal residual emotions. Clearly this was all sparked by the fear of losing my home. My fear is hooked into all the latent losses and grief that I somehow still hold, and it is interfering with my happiness. My fear really had nothing to do with the actual experience with these two agents. The fear was in me and the experience drew it out into light. I have so much to be grateful for and so much to look forward to. But I had slipped into an unconscious choice to believe in fear.

In my dream I was willing to be shot in the heart rather than live with fear. It was a portent for another leap toward the love, peace and happiness I dearly desire in a simple and free life. The reason I created LightBeam in the first place was to offer people the means to solace and wellness in natural therapies and practices. I share my own experience in such detail ("open my kimono" as George would say) to offer others some light. I've witnessed the suffering and needless tragedy of hopelessness. Sadly we live in a world that thrives on hopelessness. To rise in spite of the naysayers and find happiness is an act of will and intent.

To get to that learning, however, I needed a catalyst. My insurance broker played that part. The last words he said to me were, "You know what's going to happen? You're going to go into what they call financial depression—and then you're going to get sick!" Sweet guy. He hung up, saying, "Keep in touch." At least he had the restraint not to say, "Have a nice day."

Happiness—The Real Deal

3 of 3

Claim your bliss!

So what did I learn from that funhouse ride into the darkest part of my psyche? Well, it illustrated what I already knew, but often forget to remember. In fact, enlightenment—or I should say "practical enlightenment" (the enlightenment that is lived where we are now and not in a monastery)—is a "one step at a time" personal journey.

Most of us start out living unconsciously. As babes and young children we get our take on the world starting with the family dynamic. No news there. But what we maybe don't fully realize in this age of visualization and law of attraction is that we can read all the spiritual, self-help, and psychology books we want. We can go to sleep listening to chants or meditations; we can pray till our knees hurt, but until we actually integrate the wisdom and live it from the inside out, we will continue to be on the single rail track of our inner script.

Practical enlightenment is the process from complexity to simplicity. It is the conscious dismantling of the single rail cart that speeds us into all kinds of situations, whether we desire them or not. First we clear the debris that obscures the track and then we take it apart, one piece at a time. If we have spent decades layering one belief on top of another—beliefs and behaviors that began in our limited consciousness as babies—is it any wonder that the process of sorting and tossing becomes so onerous?

When I began my Reiki Mastery, I signed a contract agreeing to do the work and complete the process to attain the final attunement. Well, one week in I was tipped into the depths of doubt. My emotions spilled out and I was a walking bucket of uncertainty, anger, fear, and unworthiness. I called Rebecca, my Reiki Master, Dean's wife and told her that I could not continue with the program. I had made a mistake. I was not worthy to become a master of anything. I can still hear the smile in Rebecca's voice over the phone when she said, "Well, you signed a contract and it was a contract for mastery—over yourself." Always, always, always: Read the fine print!

And so began a three-year journey of witnessing the rising up and clearing out of a whole lifetime of incorrect information about myself, my divinity, my purpose, and about the workings of spirit in this world in general. It was a period that intensified my understanding of our holistic nature and really was the unfolding of the LightBeam vision. As we process from our deepest recesses, energies rise up and need to be cleared from our physical bodies. Emotional, spiritual, or psychological "work" needs to be partnered with bodywork. We need to physically clear the detritus as it rises up. It's like skimming the gunk off the top of a boiling pot of soup.

Negativity is insidious and, like a parasite, can lay dormant gaining strength for decades, only to make its appearance at unexpected times—often with cataclysmic intensity. These nasties express themselves in at least one of our bodies—physical, emotional, spiritual. They are ultimately expressed in our worldview through health, wealth, or relationship. They are not "bad" in and of themselves; they are incorrect information bytes that run the program of our beliefs and life experience. Deep beneath that morass is our true nature—the flame of our spirit—the hologram of all that we might be if we expressed our most bountiful and beautiful nature without impediment.

So we can trowel over a patina of optimism and positive thinking, and smooth it out with visualization, but unless the bedrock is firm, the cracks will return. You can be "happy" and override your default line of inner dialogue only as long as you keep talking. Eventually life will trip you up and you will be face to face with the small, frightened child of your distorted self. Either that, or like a low-grade infection, the simple pleasures of life—love and success—will be tainted with dread or doubt.

The lesson I learned over the past few days and the reason I have shared the bald truth of my own experience is a stark realization: If, in my life devoted to spiritual enlightenment and understanding, I can be walloped with the intensity that I was, then others without the benefit of perspective or practical strategies must be living lives of quiet misery. One thing has to be perfectly clear for us to proceed toward happiness. And that is: Like attracts like. You cannot, I repeat *cannot* live with doubt, fear, stress, or uncertainty and create anything other than that. And if you "think" you are living with a positive outlook and are visualizing like crazy, you will soon experience in your life what your underlying "truths" really are.

So yesterday the underlying truths revealed to me were all about loss, fear, unworthiness, and helplessness. Are they true reflections of my life? Absolutely not. What are my truths? Over these past three years I have resurrected my life from the ashes of who I used to be. I am finally witnessing the first independent steps of LightBeam as it begins to fulfill its potential to increase understanding of our holistic nature. Professionally, I am in the business of my dreams, which combines all my sensibilities, desire, and expertise in a world devoted to creativity and beauty: Art. I have gained understanding and competency in the Internet, and website function gives me full freedom from dependency. I have an unusually creative and harmonious relationship with my two sons, whom I both respect and admire. And I have a love in my life the magnitude of which is only possible because of the awareness in suffering my beloved husband's death.

So why then did the panic come up? Because there is still a script running of loss and grief that I didn't realize. Of course it found the weakness in my foundation and that was my home. Like the rest of the world, the fallout of the unexpected is affecting my freedom of action. The gathering tension of accumulated circumstances—the car, the credit, the *this*, the *that*—conspired to bring to the fore all that I need to look at closely and release. I'm in a tough spot financially. I do not know one person who is not.

The world collectively sucked in its breath in shock at the financial cataclysm nearly two years ago, and it hasn't let it out yet. Those are the facts. Those who weren't direct victims of the greed and mismanagement of other people's money—a travesty that unbelievably continues today—are in due course feeling the effects. Right now, wanting to sell my house, I have to endure a period of discomfort while the world finds a firmer footing. A friend asked a few months ago, "What are you going to do if your house doesn't sell?" Well, short of taking my two sons by the hand and gently closing the door behind us to walk into the sunset, what choice do I have but to do everything in my power to bring this to an equitable and beneficial conclusion?

I have lots of options—options that divide themselves clearly into those fuelled by fear and those fuelled by courage. The analogy that comes to mind is that I have been handed the controls of a 747 in mid-Atlantic flight. I can bail, ditch it or gather all my strength and bring it in for a landing without crashing.

The path of enlightenment is often called the path of the spiritual warrior. Practical enlightenment is the call to face your fears, find your strengths, dump the rest and claim your bliss in the simple pleasures of love, peace, and happiness—in a mansion or in a cottage. Happiness does not know money or status, but only thrives in the richness of self-awareness.

So what was all the drama about these past few days? It was my opportunity to look very closely at who I actually was. Would I bail into despondency and depression—psychological suicide? Would I ditch? Call my real estate agent or some hotshot and beg him to find a buyer, stat? The ones who are lurking in the shadows, waiting for desperate sellers? Or do I grasp responsibility? Know that I cannot function in fear, ditch that crap, and choose to focus very intently on one day at a time. Focus on my wonderful and exciting new business, representing four amazing artists. Focus on my many opportunities. Focus on my loves; focus on my strengths. My 747 carries precious cargo: My sons who are learning life skills from my every example, my dreams in all their potential, and a lifetime of memories. It's no time to panic.

The path of enlightenment has inspired my desire for a very simple life. One of beauty, creativity, vitality, serenity, love, peace, and happiness. I am going there. But first I have to land this bird!

Eden and I

Do you know the way back to peace, beauty, health, and happiness?

Today is Holy Thursday or Maundy Thursday, which I discovered is the day before Good Friday when Jesus made the symbolic gesture of washing the feet of his disciples. Tomorrow commemorates the day that He was arrested, tried, and nailed to the cross. On Sunday, millions around the world will celebrate the ascension.

When I Googled Maundy Thursday there was a litany (forgive the pun) on which Christian denomination named the day. Where the root derived through the cultural shifts of history, which nation said it first, and—for goodness sake—which calendar you might be following. And here you go: Getting distracted by the detail.

I got a card in the mail yesterday from a local church, featuring a very beautiful drawing of Jesus. His eyes are deep and lovely, personifying kindness itself. His left hand is raised gently in front of his heart in the "mudra" of peace. The headline reads, "He'd love to see you at Easter. Of course, after you've risen from the dead, you're happy to see anyone." Of a similar nature, on a huge billboard facing the highway by an enormous round evangelical church is the sign: "When Jesus returns—will you be ready?" And here you go: Getting distracted by the drama.

The detail and the drama all keep us focused on something outside of ourselves. Something from ancient history. Something experienced by another people at another time. And somehow we are supposed to go "out there" and prepare for IT, conjure the ecstasy of IT, just find IT—by being in the right place at the right time, IT will find us! Many even feel that they must suffer emotionally, spiritually, or physically in emulation of the Crucifixion before they are worthy of IT.

Sadly, as long as we look outside of ourselves we will never, may I repeat, *never* find the peace beyond understanding, nor coax the gentle dove of pure and simple goodness to rest in our hearts. It truly is not seeing the forest for the trees. The meaning behind the detail and the drama. The Crucifixion isn't about the end, of course, it is about the beginning. For us: Now. But what we seem to be missing is that the Crucifixion isn't about Jesus—it is about you and me.

Looking at this face in the photo beside me as I write, I don't see someone who would look for the spectacular. The big finish. What I see are eyes so deep and incisive that they penetrate my every illusion and barrier to that promised peace. They are the eyes of pure compassion. Eyes that know that it is through painful and startling experiences that we come to know ourselves. In the "dying" of a personal Crucifixion, we die to the judgment of others; we die to the lies we may have begun to believe about our own worth and divinity; we die to the material world as a passage to bliss; we die to the identification with our physical selves and know that our bodies will one day be cast aside like a robe in the dirt.

The morning George died, I called our sons, then 17 and 20, to the hospital where my husband and I had spent our last night together. Shortly after, his three daughters arrived and we spent several hours with him. We cried and hugged and stroked his face, sat on the bed and ate oranges, told stories. We were with him, but he had clearly "left" us. My younger son commented that, looking at the body—even of one so loved and familiar—it was clear to see that what animated it had departed and that all that remained was the husk.

I tell you this because while we may "know" we are spiritual beings having a physical experience, we don't realize or live as if we know that. We can set our own spirits free while in our physical bodies. We can experience bliss, peace, health, happiness. Right here. Right now. We don't achieve this by picking through the slim volumes of historical accounts for words to tell us what to do. We don't achieve it by debating the "real" meaning of simple words and seeking complexity.

How do we achieve peace beyond understanding? By choosing it. By choosing it over and over again until it becomes our default when thoughts of worry or self-judgment crowd our peace. By letting go of absolutely everything that does not define our true nature. And what did Jesus teach us about our true nature? That we are divine—sparks of creation from the flame of all creation in all worlds in all times—unto eternity. I'm cool with that; I just keep forgetting to remember.

You can believe me when I say I wonder at the candor of my recent writing. Why, I ask myself, am I so willing to expose my fears, my flaws, my abundant lack of poise and perfection? Sometimes I wonder if I am the only one. I write after working through a riddle of my own and feel slightly embarrassed in sharing it. After all, I am known to put stock in propriety, manners, appearances, and social etiquette. I like the idea of being in firm control of my destiny, but the world is slightly askew and I can't plan for tsunamis—personal or global. Living Life barefaced like this is more than a little untidy. But today, Maundy Thursday, I think I understand.

In my mind, if we embrace the meaning—the symbol—of the Crucifixion, we realize we are to follow the example of trust and surrender to perfect freedom. Here. Now. Do we have to die on a cross of our own construction to make that choice? Absolutely not! Is the path narrow? Yes, but not to make it difficult; to make it easy! The path leads to peace, beauty, health, and happiness. It is a path, not to Christ but *through* Christ—or Christ Consciousness—to our own divine self. Christ is not the destination, but the means to our own destiny of our highest Self. It is a path, not exclusive to Christians, of clear discernment and acts of love. What serves you and what does not. Embrace what nourishes you and discard the rest.

When we follow our heart's deepest desires we are led irrevocably to our highest Self—the fulfillment of all we have potential to offer this physical world. Are you a doctor? Teacher? Mother? Artist? Banker? Executive? Being anything but what you truly are is to wander off the path. And that leads you into the murky places of worldly judgment or the influence of unconscious sorrows. Forgive them (release them from your own judgment), because if they speak in critical judgment of others then they are out of alignment with themselves and know neither you nor themselves well enough to pass comment or to be helpful.

It is not my intention to debate religions or opine on theology. Heaven knows that there have been many historic instances—myth and fact—of virgin births, resurrection from the dead, and ascension. Why get caught in the debate? Does it matter? Don't you just want to be happy and at peace? Don't you want to know that no matter how difficult the circumstances you face, maybe they are just worldly conditions that in our surmounting them become our greatest liberators? Don't you just want to be free?

Well, you already are. Choose it. Jesus left us with the words, "Thy will be done on Earth as it is in Heaven." What do you think that means? Are we not the instruments of that Will? Is this Heaven yet? If we look for it, we will find it right where we are.

Our own minds—our analytical thoughts, our memories of pain and suffering—are our personal crosses. You can hang there pinioned until you die and are freed, or you can drop into your heart and be free now. Living through the heart is to surrender to the infinite depth of love. Love for yourself as you are now; Love for this crazy world just the way it is. It's the only one we've got. And Love for this gorgeous planet Earth. An Eden if only we would see her. Tropical beaches, rainforests, snowy mountains, golden prairies, surging oceans, flawless skies. Animals, fruits, and flowers. Butterflies. We were never cast from Eden—we looked away. Focus on the pollution and know we live in a flawed world. Focus on the beauty and know we can expand it through gentle and simple loving acts of our own divine nature.

I believe spiritual practices of any denomination can either strengthen our spiritual freedom or strangle it. Any symbolic story that takes us to the heart of our own hearts sets us free. I have found my way on many paths.

In this story, Jesus washed the feet of his disciples. An act of equality. All are children of divinity—none less or more. The story continues as Jesus surrendered in trust and illuminated a way to peace on Earth—seeds in our own hearts. If we choose, we can find the true meaning and begin to live Heaven on Earth and reclaim Eden.

If You Never Lie

…You never have to remember what you said.

My father taught me that. Handy advice. My dad had many neat sayings that were bite sized pieces of advice—some his own and some, I'm sure, from his parents. He also told me that when people end a sentence with "Honest!" they have just told you a lie. The other thing he warned me about—and I seem to keep forgetting—is that we tend to assume that others live by the same rules of conduct we do. In other words, if we don't use deceit as a viable means to an end, then we don't expect others to. And the giant one: If people lie about the little things then they *definitely* lie about the big things!

Why am I sharing this? Because I keep getting slapped by lies and deceit. Am I a magnet for this? Apparently so. Am I naive? Not so much. What am I doing about it? Well, a little bit at a time. My dad also taught me about honor and dignity and noble acts. His word was his bond and all "deals" sealed with a handshake.

Hibbie Bull said what he meant and he did what he said he would do. Life was simple. He told me one time that the owner of the company he represented asked him to lie to a customer. He refused to do it, explaining to the owner, "If I will lie *for* you I will lie *to* you. You will never be able to trust me again."

Me? I have buckets of trust. So much so that I keep pouring it into the hands of those who do not deserve it. Am I stupid? No. I deeply desire to live in a world that is based on trust and accountability. I will continue to act from my highest values. It is the only way that the fabric of human goodness that has been so torn over the past decades can ever be repaired. How do I do that?

Well, after my recent adventure when I tripped and bruised myself over caveat emptor, Athan, my mate and, sometimes, life interpreter explained it this way: If I, and others like me, desire to live in a world based on the Golden Rule, then we must realize the statistics. We are in the minority. That means if there are 5% of us on the planet living and doing business under these criteria and expectations, then 95% are not. Ergo, the majority of the people and businesses we deal with will be trying to take advantage of us, slipping something under the radar, or plain out lying. The rub is that because this practice is so rife, it has become the new norm. Lies and deceit are written right into contracts. They are legal—but are they ethical? No, no, no, and NO!

The thing my dad forgot to mention, and maybe it didn't apply so much then, was that the truth does *not* always win out. Often—way too often—the nefarious guys win. They are good at what they do, they prepare for the battle, and they have deep pockets. They have no moral compass, so any means are justified to achieve their end. They set out to deceive in the first place—that was the goal—so they create their modus operandi around that. For instance, they know that human nature is to look up to the right when we lie (or the other way round, depending on whether you are left or right-handed), so they look you straight in the eye. They overcome their basic human nature on oh so many levels.

My most recent handful? The cell phone company arbitrarily cancelled my program when my son got his new iPhone. They charged me two thousand dollars over two months. Because it was paid automatically (trust) I now have to fight to get my money back. I have sent a lawyer's letter—which if you have seen the film *Avatar* is like sending a feathered arrow across the bow of the mothership.

On another occasion, another phone company kept charging me for a business line and Internet for two years after I had cancelled the service and closed my boutique. I had played ping pong on the phone with operators from Halifax to Quebec until I had had enough of dreaming they might have any interest in customer service other than to wear me down until I gave up. I finally wrote to the two vice presidents in charge of each service and copied CRTC. Problem solved.

A security alarm company wrote in the term of my contract—five years—after I had signed it. At the time I was renting a store with a two-year lease. I read that contract before I signed it and know unequivocally that I would not sign a five-year contract in a two-year property. Why would I? It was "handwritten" in two places. I would have seen it. Could I prove it? Nope. Result: I had to pay. Fortunately two years after the fact the new tenant took on the contract and my obligation was complete.

And contractors? Well, suffice it to say that people like Mike Holmes have thriving renovation rescue shows because of the code of conduct of building subcontractors. Getting work done is a little like a survivor show. In the past I have made it my specialty to attract the lowest of the low. Even though they came recommended, and didn't know each other, they all more or less had the same scheme. Come in, tear their corner of the house apart and then, with all the debris lying in the middle of the floor and the ceiling open to the heavens say, "Oh, just one thing…I'm not going to be able to finish the job for the original price I quoted." You can't even share this grief with your friends because they will invariably have a similar story.

When did this get so out of control? I am shamed by my own willingness to pay to make things right, thinking that in the end they would do a good job because they really meant well. Actually they never did mean well. The bottom of the ninety-fifth percentile contains these characters. The lesson? Check references and go and see work for yourself. Disregard the voice of polite conditioning that tells you it is suspicious and not respectful or trusting of others.

My most recent one is very interesting. Just yesterday, I discovered I had dropped into a snake pit. They are many and I am one. They have a reputation for coercion and litigation. Wrongful contracts written by clever lawyers—teeny tiny print. Their way of doing business is to impale clients on automatic contract renewals and then litigate when the client tries to cancel or challenges the contract. (My case is more heinous, the details of which are not relevant here.) The cases they win are those where the client doesn't show up for the trial in the US. They boast of their client list, and clients of that caliber can afford to write off a bad situation rather than send someone to court to play against a stacked deck.

I have two things going against me to choose that action, if it comes to that. One: I do not owe the money. Two: My business motto is Better Business through Conscious Action. I will not perpetuate the wellbeing of a company that uses coercion to prosper. I cannot. If I have to borrow the money I will do so. I may only be one—but I intend to be a very loud "one." Even if I "lose" I will win.[3]

The other thing that Athan told me which I didn't so much want to hear is that the 5%—once they grasp the lay of the land—must not only be forewarned and protect themselves, but more importantly for the future of this world must also be prepared to stand up against the 95%. I would prefer to will a beautiful world and let my desires make it so. But to paraphrase Dr. Phil—that's not working so well for me.

So what do we do when "they" have more power, more lawyers, more money, and more tricks than we do? We pick up one tiny stone and aim it very, very well. I'm not sure what I will do yet, but once I decide

---

[3] When I wrote this post the company in question read it and asked me to take it down. I refused because it named no names. I never heard from them again. Sigh…the phone companies continue to outwit me.

I will put it out to the others of the 5% and gather a following. If you are reading this now, I mean you. What will I ask of you? Just be there as my witness. As Margaret Mead said, "Never doubt that a small group of thoughtful, committed citizens can change the world. Indeed, it is the only thing that ever has."

Awash in Lemonade

And the great rubber band remedy.

Do you remember the *I Love Lucy* episode when Lucy and Ethel get a job in the chocolate factory? At first they manage to keep up with the conveyor belt and then, as it gets faster, they miss a few, pocket a few and finally end up shoving handfuls of chocolates into their mouths until they are sick. Well, it might be okay at the outset to make lemonade when life hands you lemons, but in the long run all you end up with is a sticky mess that doesn't quench your thirst! Also, as your boat floats off course on a sweet and yellow sea, you are so busy with processing lemons that you take your eye off the horizon—your goal—while your charts blur.

Before you get sick of the lemonade analogy, bear with me a second more. There are two worlds we live in: The Big Picture and the Little Drama. We are always straddling them, probably while Heaven looks on taking bets. Which will we choose? Will we choose to be free and fulfill our most gorgeous, joyful, creative selves and live in community with other such individuals? Will we get distracted by all the lemons lobbed at us, consumed by the mundane and live a life making the best of sour situations—relationships, jobs, finances, the world?

Many years ago, I had an epiphany. My role in life was to create beauty, peace, harmony—a world of loveliness—health, vitality, joy, and creativity. Let's call it Eden. I didn't at the time know how I was going to do this exactly, but I knew that there were plenty of people bent on ugliness, hate, war, greed, and abuse, and even more people who live unconsciously—not even knowing they have choices. They shrug their shoulders, shake their collective head, and squeeze more lemons.

There are the terrorists, over there, igniting child suicide bombers with visions of the afterlife; there is the war machine, down there, which niftily keeps its populace distracted from the essentials lacking in such a resource rich society; there are bankers, everywhere, who play us like marionettes—yanking hundreds of thousands off their feet by playing shell games with their very life savings. And then there is the Big Pharma and the WHO, which short of killing us, thrive on continued illness of the body or malaise of the spirit. And the charge that runs through the wires of all that terror and uncertainty is the ubiquitous voice of the media.

I admit there might have been a thread of a rant in my recent writing. But it wasn't until I witnessed someone close to me shedding the skin of a persona that was familiar but no longer served them, that I got the "aha" moment. As one listening to another as they stand shivering and vulnerable before new skin forms, I remembered what I have experienced so many times before. And that is: Just as you are about to take a leap into an uncharted and sparkling lagoon of self-actualization, you absolutely must shed all that does not serve you. Fear, doubt, insecurity, negativity, attachment—all—gotta go!

The parable about the camel, the rich man, and the eye of the needle isn't about wealth keeping you from Heaven—it is that often wealth or some other form of attachment is a compensation for insecurity or lack of self-esteem that is hard to let go. We become attached to our stuff—our possessions, our relationships, our status, our "good" name. We think it protects us from an uncertain world. But all this stuff and status is the construct of the world described above—the Little Drama.

Ironically this Little Drama plays out over and over again on a global scale. It affects the collective soul of humanity where millions of children starve on a planet that would supply our every need and desire if we didn't hoard, modify, pollute or kill her bit by bit in our ignorance and avarice. This nightmare is largely driven by those whose agenda is self-serving, and peopled by the mostly unconscious and unquestioning.

I'm not unconscious but sometimes I forget to remember. While I'm ranting about *them*, I'm not doing anything constructive about *me*. While I am busy making lemonade, my boat is slipping into the fast current with the others that are heading for the falls. Remember Marilyn Monroe in *Niagara*? Man, that movie scared me! How do you get back to the Big Picture and out of the slipstream of unconsciousness? Well, with a rubber band.

In the world of the Little Drama you are playing against the house which business it is to win—at all costs. They know all the odds and angles and play them, for survival—their survival, not yours, and not the world's. For a moment you might win a bit, even become intoxicated with the glamour and bright lights, but in the long run, you lose. This game isn't about money or security: It is about *freedom*. The game is a losing game as long as you are kept distracted and uncertain—busy making lemonade, like a good little stoic, or Baptist, or Muslim, or New Ager.

The rubber band? Oh yes. In this world bent on uncertainty, it is said the average person has an insecure or negative thought six or seven times an hour! If we know that we cannot plant a peach tree and grow an elephant, then we know, absolutely, that we reap what we sow. So if we have negative and insecure thoughts six or seven times an hour (more in the wee hours, from experience), how can we create a life of joy and abundance?

We can visualize and have all the pictures we want of our hearts' desires (Greek villas on the Aegean anyone?) but if we continue with unexamined mental activity, how close are we going to get to our dream? And what is our dream but an expression of all that we have in us to be? The ultimate fulfillment of our own perfect and unique Self, living in beautiful surroundings with people we love, creating a world of happiness?

Just as I came upon the negative thought statistic, I did a little self-analysis quiz in a book. The book said to get someone who knows you well to help. So I asked Athan. I had answered the questions with my impeccable self-awareness and honesty, and just wanted him to affirm my clarity.

The first question was, "Are you mostly positive or negative?"

"Positive, of course," say I.

"Ha!" says Athan.

"What?" I rejoin, incredulous and terribly hurt.

"Well, you get there eventually—but you sure don't start there," Athan smiled.

Tearing up, I said, "Well then, what right do I have writing about awareness if I'm so negative?"

"See what I mean?" my beloved replied gently.

When I shared this with my friend, she suggested I put a rubber band around my wrist, and every time I have a negative thought—snap it. Well, after the shock of the irrefutable fact that I default to negativity more than a little, you know what I discovered? First of all that snapping rubber bands hurts like hell. Second, people close to you think that it's okay to snap your band for you if you miss a random comment. Third, I discovered a lot of the negative and insecure thoughts are not even my own! They are from sources beyond memory, from the news, from other peoples' opinions, and reflections of a very warped world. In short, our thoughts keep us tethered to the world of the Little Drama. And in the Little Drama we are inevitably small and our dreams pinched and beyond reach.

The fourth and most important thing I learned? When I control my thoughts—every one of them—the lemons don't keep hurtling at me. And when I stop making lemonade, there is no sea; there are no rapids, no falls. My goal—freedom—Eden—lies shining on the horizon and the way is on solid ground. In my hands right now is all I need to create the life I desire. In my heart is the hologram of all that I might be. So today I will concentrate on all the positive and constructive thoughts and actions I can take toward my own freedom. And what if I get snagged on the opinion of others, the wish for security over independence, or fear of the unknown? I'll just snap out of it!

Let the Bells Ring Out—I Get It!

The law of garbage.

In the middle of the night when I am wont to wake, I sometimes surface with those trailing tendrils of prophetic dreams. Last night, the dream was about searching for a job of a certain description. I was using search terms similar to those I had used a year before and found that the jobs that came up were the same as the previous year. Not only that, they seemed to have a similar feeling of negativity. Curious. How could they still be open, I wondered? Then I realized these were different jobs entirely but matched my search nonetheless. The negativity was somehow part of my criteria and the dissatisfaction of the result commensurate to my lack of expectation.

Then WHAM! Lights! Bells! I got it! I knew it all along—repeated it to myself like a mantra and still didn't get the significance and sublime simplicity of THE LAW. What law? The Law of Attraction? Nope. Simpler. More real and grounding (literally) than the Law of Gravity. What is it? The LAW of GARBAGE! Yep! Garbage In = Garbage Out.

The thing is, I've been working on a book called *Making Friends with the Sky: The Chicken Little Guide to the Internet.* In it I share my discovery, as I drop deeper into web design, Internet marketing, traffic trends, and search engines, about the very nature of the Internet. That the Internet is a model for consciousness. In short, it is our precursor or teacher for the rate and subtlety of communication and creative manifestation that we have been promised for centuries.

Of all the prophets and spiritual leaders, many used the simple language of parable so that the lessons on how the universe works as a creative vehicle driven on Love could be easily understood by all—educated and simple alike. A mustard seed. A lily. We seem continually bent on looking past the obvious in search of a more complex solution to the woes of Life on Earth. We stand on the headland of Life and are buffeted by the winds of change and whimsy. Life seems to be what happens to us.

And then this morning came the revelation. So clear. So simple. So provable. The books all say to be specific in your intentions. To write down your goals—repeat them over and over. If you want a car, name the model. If you want a successful income, name the amount. If you want a great relationship, describe the very qualities you desire. Why? I used to think it was to train my mind or somehow forge a bridge between my desires and the universe so the universe could get busy and manifest it. If I repeated it enough I would finally believe it and then the universe would provide it.

Then I'd get caught up in what was "right" for me. What was the divine plan? What was my role in creation? If I got what I thought I wanted, would I be happy? Would it be "good" for everyone around me? And while I was grunting and fretting through consciousness, the rest of the world was either doing the same or more often, careening through life, banging into people and circumstances beyond their control. And there's a good word: Control. How many of us think we have to control the outcome to get what we desire?

So what is this epiphany? What is so sublimely simple and obvious that I had to climb up and lumber over it every minute of every day while I looked for the light? Well it is this: You get what you ask for. Right, you say. We know this. "Ask and it shall be given." "Be careful what you wish for." Of course. I ask…but do I get? Sometimes. Mix emotion with your request—it makes it happen faster, like fuel on the fire of desire. Is that right? Maybe, but not for the reasons I thought.

I had my list of wishes and I'd ramp up my emotions—first to overwhelm my emotions of doubt, fear and anxiety, and then to fire up the excitement for...what? Harmony? Success? A villa in the sun? My business? Love? Peace? Happiness? Cool. Now, let me show you a simple little illustration using the Internet to model how the universe manifests. Interested? I think you will be if you get what I get.

When I Google my desires, here are my search results:

Harmony: 61,000,800

Success: 311,000,000

Villa in the sun: 34,300,000

Business: 1,600,000,000

Love: 1,350,000,000

Peace: 244,000,000

Happiness: 69,800,000

Now let me get a little more specific: "For sale traditional stone villa in Hydra Greece three bedroom, terrace overlooking Kamini Harbor walk to beach..." Now watch this...search results? 101. In case it's not yet clear, think about this. How long would it take me to find what I want if I have to go through thirty-four million, three hundred thousand websites? Would I give up before I got to the last page of junk? Now that I have 101, I can fine-tune that still more until I have a short list. Then, once my house sells—I'm outta here!

So it's not about repetition. It's not about emotion. It's not about "good" or "bad." It's not about "conjuring" a result from the universe by will or intent. It is about specific and clear directions. No more. No less. No garbage (unless trash is what you seek). The clearer the vision, the more specifics given—the faster the circumstances can be met. There are fewer matches and so you and the love of your life can find each other because neither of you will be bothering with the dross of wasted time and emotion in the wrong relationships. The life you want cannot be left to chance. Period. And doubt? You don't have time!

I've had random experiences of this and called it synchronicity. But now I get it. Emotion is important—not for the level of passion—but for the detail passion gives you. I want to live on Hydra because Leonard Cohen lived and loved and wrote poetry there; artists and authors cluster there; and by chance (hmm) a photo I cut out of *Architectural Digest* in the 1990s that has helped me get through my toughest times, I discovered recently, is looking over Kamini Harbor from the terrace of the McGuire (furniture design) family villa. Now is it too much to imagine that the man in my life is, what? Greek, maybe? *Coincidentally* (did I say that out loud), two friends chatting at my husband George's funeral wondered what would happen next. One said to the other, "Oh, she'll probably end up on an island in Greece, writing a book."

My mistake has been to see will and intention as a jaw set, hands on hips determination to manifest—dammit! To rake off the weeds on the top of the water until your dream glimmers up from the depths. But now I see that you can't even think about the weeds, let alone engage in raking them. Google search for weeds: 70,500,000. If I put "weeds" and "Greece" in the search I'm going to get a lot about Dandelions, which has nothing to do with where I want to live when I kick this pop stand. Mixing up our search gets results but they are garbled and unsatisfactory. My own ambiguity has cluttered my path on many fronts.

I've got to tell you, it was the rubber band that did it. Once I started being aware of all the moments I give energy and focus to negative or insecure thoughts, I got closer to this realization. When your mind is not engaged in all the garbage that can, might, is, did, or will go down, there is finally room for sunshine thoughts. It's easier to fill in the details and get specific about disaster, disease, discord, and distrust because we are constantly pummeled with the message in both our news and "entertainment." Turn it off. Turn your desires on. Sketch out your desire and then fill in the details. Very clearly. Be specific. Cut out pictures. Add music. Daydream about a conversation in these circumstances.

Think about it. If impulses of light traveling on fiber optics can connect you instantly with your cousin in Saudi, or allow you to purchase a $55,000 painting on eBay, can Creation Itself not tumble Paradise at your feet for the asking?

And what about God? The divine plan? When you are fulfilling your desires and the outcome is your happiness, then the world will follow you and will be a happier place. It cannot be otherwise. Look at the stats. It's easy to see where the global "head" is. War, 800 million, outweighs Peace, 244 million, by nearly 4:1. So if your head is your computer and the universe (collective unconscious, according to Jung) is the Internet, what are you putting into your search? Every single choice you make gets a result. When you don't make choices—clear and definitive— you get the world of spam; everybody else's uncensored, unconscious, unclear, noise and confusion.

Now that you get it too, rather than life happening to you—make sure you happen to Life!

Finding Your Pole Star

From here I can see forever.

Ever see the truck commercial where the vehicle is sitting at the tippy top of a rock overlooking the entire Arizona Painted Desert, with red rock buttes overlooking the 360° horizon? Did you wonder what it might be like to be at the top of your world and have a panorama of possibility?

I'm there right now. It's new so I'm feeling a little wobbly in the moment. Gravity is also 360° and tugs at my bare toes, clinging to the craggy outcrop. I am alone. Unencumbered. I have sold my home and in mere days—sixty, no, fifty-seven—the shell that has protected my sons and me will slip away. My young musicians will follow the notes to their own bliss. My mate stands on his own mountaintop, over there. We see each other but do not stand side by side…yet.

It is time to be me. To walk through these rooms and halls and, with a critical eye, choose of my possessions as wisely as one embarking on Samadhi. Like rings in a tree, furniture and things reflect the growing circles of life; through infancy—the toys, the sheepskin, and English pram; through youth—desks, soccer trophies, brightly-colored goalkeeper shirts; through maturity—my own—heart and soul. The ebb and flow, births and death, gain and loss. Always climbing toward the place where I can see.

So much of life is lived responding and reacting to the moving picture of family played against the backdrop of society, overlaid on the screen on the globe itself. It seems I've gone way out in life—learning, building, acquiring, and now am receding, letting all that I accumulated in stuff and memory tumble onto the beach to pick up like precious shells, or let it be drawn back into the deep of life experience forgotten. But here I am—to stand alone. Unencumbered. Choosing which direction to take. To the villa in Greece? I hear there are no trees on some islands. To the Caribbean islands? Maybe.

But wait! What are these little tendrils of light that flow from my heart? My sons are young men and must set out on their own hero's journeys, but for the moment I am their pole star. In time that star will fade and they will find a brighter guiding light—their own. For the moment I must be still so they can find me if they need to. I won't be down the hall when they flop on the end of the bed and chat about their night out. Until they are too busy to call, I want to be in the vicinity.

Evolving as a mature family is like dividing the roots of a large perennial. Above the ground individual shoots find the sun, but below is an entwined mass of sustenance and nourishment. A caring gardener will dig well beyond the root ball and then gently disengage the roots until they dangle free and unharmed, ready to be replanted in a fertile space for optimum growth. In our particular tangle of roots are those enlivening bits of George that remain part of each of us. They are the confidence and wisdom in one, and the easy leadership and fun in the other. And in me, a willingness to love myself. Leaving this house of childhood, youth, happiness, celebration, illness, and death is this very untangling. There will inevitably be pockets of pain, tears, and memory. There will also be the excitement of new adventure. The giddiness of expectation that Life is full of infinite possibility. "And a motorcycle," says one prince.

Infinite possibility. Yes. Standing here at the top of the world, where I can see forever. What is it I truly desire? Ironically, now that I am here in my perspective, I realize that we are, all of us, here always—we just don't know it. We encumber ourselves with stuff that is chained to the economic leviathan. Our possessions and our roles are tied to the tail of a beast of the ocean depths. When it submerges, we go under—into the dark unknown, holding our breath until the beast swings skyward and thrusts back up through the surface. Propelled by its massive tail, the beast flings itself through the air and we hold on—swinging midair, still holding our breath—bracing again for the plummet beneath the surface. We never quite touch down with our feet on the solid ground of our own purpose and desire.

When do we breathe? When do we sleep? When do we create? When do we live the life we were born to live? When we let go. "For every purpose there is a season." There is a time to grow and accumulate, and a time to scatter seeds. Many of us do not live by the natural rhythms of human nature. We live hanging onto the tail of the monster that is fed by all the random emotions of a society that believes that safety lies outside of our hearts. As long as this belief persists as the foundation of our economic and cultural actions, we will create edifices of our minds. No matter how big or glamorous or rich they may appear, they are of the stuff of inevitable disintegration.

As long as we look outside of ourselves for protection and safety and peace of mind, we will be assessed and found worthy or wanting based on our contribution to the edifice of the mind. The values of the human animal as gregarious and kind are neither rate-able nor marketable, so they are not "valued." I was speaking to a friend a few days ago who said that he has decided to downsize his business and just do projects that he really desires. He went on to say that when he started in business thirty years ago, one could rely on a handshake. Now, he said, even a contract is worthless.

Honor, honesty, goodness, compassion, trust, integrity, and kindness are values that hold little appeal to the world of the moment. Goodness is for suckers and there is a sucker born every minute. Meanwhile, those who would lure them into the chains of the leviathan are many. Like in *The Matrix*, the ones that mean to steal your freedom wear suits. You can choose to avoid neighborhoods or types that look menacing, they advertise their dark side, but the others are far more dangerous and nefarious. In a way the "crooks" bash you over the head and steal your money or your car, but the "suits" offer you the world in exchange for what is most precious (freedom), and hitch you to the tail.

Many years ago, during the recession of the 1980s, George and I required an extension on our line to cover payroll on a big contract. At one of the high-rise offices in Toronto, the bank officer replied to George's charge of usury—40% interest—by saying, "Look at it this way: You get to keep your business, your home and your wife. But if you lose everything, she'll probably leave you." I remember that moment well because I too was sitting in that meeting, pregnant with our first child. "Where do I sign?" George replied. We rode that beast and succeeded in several other businesses thereafter, in spite of the hobbles of other people's agendas.

I am no stranger to challenges—financial, psychological, or emotional. They have strengthened me and honed my skills. Most importantly (and I kind of wish it didn't take so long), they have cleared my vision of what is important and what is not. What frees me and what enslaves me. I have been naughty because I have not "played the game." I have not supported the matrix. My most recent experience, to which I will give no energy in sharing, is rocking the very foundations of my maternal and survival instincts. The "suits" come in close and you let them in because you were raised to trust them, and they hold what is dear to you (your means of survival). Then they look you in the eye as they sucker punch you in the solar plexus.

For those who know their chakras—the solar plexus is the center of personal will and self-esteem. When we place power outside of our personal jurisdiction, we react to the dramas of life. Responding to life seems a more structured, reasonable, and conventional way to live. It may get crazy but at least you're up against something that draws your response—in courage or awareness. But who or what do we choose to react to? There is the word: Choose. This is the freedom we don't have to wait until we are at the top of the world to experience. Exerting our personal will is our freedom. Once gaining that freedom, I vow to protect it to my death.

Does that mean I am going to live outside of the mainstream? Not at all. As long as we see the mainstream as a vehicle to personal will and freedom, and not as a substitute, it can provide our livelihood and support our personal choices. Freedom for me is an oasis of serenity, natural beauty, breezes, sunlight; a gathering place for those I love and respect; a place of creation. Freedom is unhitching from the leviathan. Freedom is *willing* freedom and then dropping all constraints and attachments that are not of the heart. As I pivot with a 360° view, which direction will I take? It doesn't matter. I have already arrived in my heart and I am my own pole star.

The Free Range of Business

The intrinsic nature of business.

What do free-range chickens, Jack Russell terriers and the color beige have to do with the intrinsic nature of business? Well, this: Every particle of the universe—be it animal, vegetable, or mineral, or even manmade—has a nature of its own and unique characteristics of behavior.

This morning, pre-coffee, Athan and I were talking about the potential move to a new house. We joked about how the standalone screened room would make an excellent chicken coop and we could make our fortune breeding free-range chicks. I told Athan that we used to have free-range chickens—Rhode Island Reds—the whole wheat of chickens, if you will, on our farm when we first moved to King City. The problem with free range is that weasels are also free range and it is *their* nature to "ferret" out chickens and tear out their little throats.

Athan opined that clearly our dogs weren't tough protectors. Not so much. Golden Retrievers are bred to be soft-mouthed, obedient, and, if not brilliant, uncompromisingly happy and silly! And our Siberian Husky was just an adventuress always looking for the way across the fence. On the other hand, breeds like Jack Russells and most of the terriers are fearless. They chase anything moving despite its size—like Mack Trucks; they're barky to the extreme—so as to be found by the farmer after they had tunneled down badger burrow; and, in many cases, more cunning than humans give the cute little things credit for as they shove them in a pink Burberry puppy carrier!

It is when we try to homogenize everything or categorize according to face values that we weave ourselves a life of discontent at best, and disaster of global proportions at worst. The funnel of the mass commercial market—which includes banks, retailers, insurance companies, governments, media, manufacturers—mixes all things bright and beautiful and makes beige—a color that doesn't really exist in nature. A shade—perhaps neutral but really synonymous with boring or dull—that is stultifying, like concrete.

Years ago Muzak got a bad rap (no pun intended). Elevator music was dull, dull, dull—ironically to the point of becoming annoying. Today's music is equally formulaic; a blend of rap, dance, techno and EMO that slops all over us from most pop radio stations. A band gets a hit and writes the same song over and over again. Why do they do that? Because it is a known commodity and presents no risk in repetition. The market wants what is familiar. Ricky Nelson sang about it in 'Garden Party'.

I am a voracious reader of all things—business, spiritual, and fiction in between. What I have watched is that the demand for known authors to continue to produce known products has diluted quality work readily available in the big box stores. What started out as well-crafted novels by excellent writers has diminished by books hurried through the creative process to feed the hungry maw of the ordinary. I feel for the writers. Unless they are tired of eating, they get locked into the mediocrity machine.

Quality trained artists of distinction—if they are still alive—must compete with those who may express themselves artistically but not necessarily creatively. Not all children playing a two-finger version of 'Heart and Soul' on the piano are Mozart—no matter our parental bias. Facebook, Flickr and camera phones have blurred the impact of photographic art. Allegory and storytelling reduced to cartoon. "Here's me with Ted." "Here's me drunk." "Here's me when Ted opened the bathroom door." The intimate and sensational? Boring. Dull.

Is it our nature to be voyeurs? Exhibitionists? I don't think so. I think it is our nature to be individuals and express that in our choices. I think that in our over stimulation, we can't be stimulated at all. What's a marketer to do? What is the next rage (pun intended)? When our whole commercial edifice is invested in beige—what next? The irony is that we are being teased into thinking we are individuals by documenting in blog and photo every nuance of our every day. "Navel gazing," my mother would have called it. It seems to me that culturally we are being troweled over by a layer of beige as deadening as concrete.

If the suffocation of the creative spirit isn't bad enough, let's look at the deadening of our waters, air, and soil. Our pseudo consciousness of carbon credits and endless global agenda to plan to meet to discuss… merely means that if I promise to plant a tree, I can still pollute your water. Air? There's lots of it. It's everywhere. I see conscientious joggers on city streets breaking a sweat and sucking in lungs full of toxins—only to be outraged when products aren't pure and natural.

One such woman insisted that she wanted a simple regimen with pure products, for which she'd happily pay a premium. "I just want to splash water on my face in the morning and put on a moisturizer I can trust, because it only contains 'thus and so'." Little does she know that, unless she's running to her fridge every morning for her face cream, it contains a whole lot more than 'thus and so'—otherwise she would be spreading her face with bacteria and mold (also natural, to be fair).

Years ago when we leased our farm out for crops, we chose to stay away from high-yielding corn crops because between over-cultivation and the use of Atrazine, the soil inevitably is depleted and must then lie fallow sometimes for years before regaining its nutrients. Even worse, it affects the cycle of "good" insects and creatures, which are interdependent. An interdependence that is less about "them", the creatures and insects, and more about "us." Yesterday, I signed a petition to preserve the wild and domestic honeybee habitat. Our bees are dying, which means the natural and holistic (pollen from many sources) reproduction is impeded.

Big Farm (as opposed to Big Pharma) is just as frightening is its monopoly on crop production of our prairies—you know "the bread basket," the food belt? Genetically modified crops require genetically appropriate chemicals to even get a seed to grow in otherwise dead land. The soil? Completely dependent on chemical intervention to produce. If there are not balanced and "wholesome" (meaning including the natural spectrum) nutrients in the soil, what is the value of the food to our bodies beyond being filler? And worse, what imbalance or dependence is it creating within our bodies? We are, after all, what we eat.

This isn't a rant about all that is going wrong, but a call to all who wish to set things right. It is not the fault of business. Business and commerce is the supply of all the products and services that support life on Earth. Food, clothing, transportation, homes, healthcare. The intrinsic nature of business is fair exchange. A producer offers a product of quality and value for a fair price. A buyer supports that continued production of quality products or services of value by paying a fair price, and continuing to do so in his purchasing discernment and expectation. Laissez-faire and competition assures that "natural" selection and process.

Corporations pandering to governments to protect a monopoly, financial institutions manipulating the very instruments of commerce, and institutions breeding beige are completely nihilistic of the intrinsic nature of business. So…what is the good news?

This: Human nature has prevailed and has found its path of flourishing through the Internet. Through micro markets. The same Internet, you might ask me, that contains pornography, racism, and recipes for bombs? Yep! Because it also illumines the spirit, consciousness, and individuality of men and women. It illustrates in its trillion pinpoints of fiber optics that we are all one and interdependent, and that our every choice is recorded and accountable. Just ask Google. Ask Amazon. They will tell you what book you might like, based on what you chose before. They will tell you where you are likely to go in the future, based on past decisions. Don't like the direction? Back to you. Change it. Choose differently. The world of commerce will respond to you. Money is exchange. Every dollar you spend is a vote for or against personal freedom, clean air, pure water, nourishing food. Through our conscientious purchases, we can bring the monster of the mass market to its knees. We can break beige into a kaleidoscope, one dollar at time. *That* is the intrinsic nature of business.

The Black Hole of Indecision

How dark is it inside a cow's stomach?

When I was little we summered at the cottage—a log cabin on top of a granite rock. When we came home late in the evening from some event, we would feel our way up the sloping granite, one footfall at a time, following the bouncing beam of a flashlight.

The whip-poor-wills and crickets would be raucous, and the stars sparkling overhead. I would cling to my dad's hand and he would declare: "It's as dark as the inside of a cow's stomach!" I used to think that was a riot—but I don't just now.

It's 2:45AM. Son number two is watching *Chinatown*—his dad's all-time favorite movie. Son number one is making ginger and lemon tea to soothe his strep throat. Last night they auditioned for a record label. They are on their way. In exactly one month from now we won't be chatting in the kitchen in the middle of the night—we won't be here at all. Where we will be has yet to be determined.

Who I will be is the question. All external descriptors will cease to be and I will be alone. The black hole is not a hole of despair—although it is a bit scary—it is like the black of outer space; infinite possibility. I can go anywhere and be anything. But can I, really? I am technically divested of active motherhood, home ownership. Widowed three years ago, I am nobody's wife. I have my own business so I don't belong to a company or have a title. Okay, that's all that I am not, but what am I then?

At various workshops over the years groups have participated in the "Who are you" exercise. Partnered off with a stranger, you whisper in her ear, "Who are you?" and she must answer the first thing that comes to mind: "Mother," for instance. You keep asking until there are no more "definitions" and then the truth emerges: Light, Love. Whatever. And then you go home. Home. Home.

A week ago today, I said to my agent (and friend), "Let's buy a house today." I knew the one and was eager to put in the offer. "Before you do," said my agent, "I want to show you all that I can find with your criteria. Then you can make the final decision." He then showed me a house even better—all the check marks—property, privacy, nature, light, openness, spaciousness, beauty—and best of all, in my own neighborhood. A new home!

I was ecstatic. I called Son number two to come up right away. He loved it! There was room if they wanted to come home for a visit and a great kitchen for them to create their wonderful meals. (It was our standing joke since we sold the house that they would have to come home once a month so that I would eat well.) The next day, Son number one and Athan came to see it. They loved it too. It was declared so "me!" Back home, we had coffee on the deck and started talking about the particulars of the offer. I could feel myself slipping into a very odd funk.

My oldest was giving me strange looks and finally asked for a private moment. Off we went to the laundry room. I was leaning against the washing machine and he was perched atop a ubiquitous load of laundry.

"The house is everything you want," he said. "Time is running out. Just buy it! Yesterday you were so happy and now you are glum. What's up?"

I told him the truth, as I knew it: I didn't know.

Athan and I went to the boat for the long weekend to gain some perspective. A vast lake and broad blue sky is great for that. I felt overwhelmed by everyone's well-meaning advice, but felt each had his or her own personal connection to the outcome. I phoned a good friend and, sitting on a bench overlooking the marina, had a heart-to-heart. "Picture yourself waking up in the morning, three years from now," advised my friend. "What do you see out the window?" I saw it—ocean—but how do I get there from here? I felt better, but in the middle of the night, in the tiny V berth, I awoke with stomach wrenching anxiety and kneeled on the mattress with my head in my hands. I just couldn't buy a house! My checklist was based on where I had been, not where I was going! And where *was* that, exactly? What ocean? I knew that if I was *that* conflicted, the decision was clear and that was to rent until I stepped out of the old skin of mother, chatelaine, and into a sense of who I might become—where I was no longer defined by external circumstance. Accepting that uncertainty, I slept.

In the morning I said to Athan that I thought I might be having a midlife crisis. "I think you absolutely *should* have one—before you make any big decisions," he replied. We went sailing that evening and watched the blue of the sky merge with the blue of the lake as the sun lowered in the sky. I was as calm as the water, which is near perfect sailing weather for me. One knot—no heeling.

Fast forward to today: We're looking for houses to rent. Athan is on the Internet—Craig's List. I called an agent and when she asked what area, I said anywhere west of Yonge Street to St. Catharines, Highway 9 in the north to the Lake in the south. I'd like property, but it could be in a subdivision—and I have two dogs. I explained I was in transition and just wanted a couple of months to get my bearings. I was flexible, but particular.

It was a turbulent day. Each time Athan made a suggestion, I became more and more sullen. This guy didn't know me at all. And if *he* didn't, who did? And that was the rub. We drove around and looked at subdivisions, and I got cranky while he got irritated. Then we went for gelato. Sitting on the patio with the breeze blowing, rhapsodizing over mango, peach, and lychee, and letting the Friday night traffic get on, Athan asked me what was underlying my crankiness.

"Just the fact that you don't know me at all, and what sort of place I'd be happy in," I began.

"Oh, no. This is not about me," he said, "it is about you." (Will this guy let up?) "You are not very clear on precisely where or what you do want, but when you see what you don't want, some dark emotion comes up and you project the anger onto me. What is that underlying emotion?"

What indeed? My chin trembled and giant hot tears began to cascade. I put on my sunglasses. Who is that behind the Ray Bans? Damned if I know—but she's soggy. Here I am, as free to be and do whatever I desire as any time in my life, and I am terrified. I'm afraid of "leaving home." If I go and fulfill my long stated desires, where will I come home to? If I set out on my dream, where will I bring my world-weary body back to? Where is my bed, my room, my door to close and be quiet; my own safe place? Why did that scare me so much? What was my sense of safety hooked to? Is "home" a place, a protective shell, or a state of being?

Last evening over tea, Athan read me the five stages of midlife crisis—Jung-esque. Here they are in italics, my interpretation following:

Accommodation—meeting other's expectations, our roles, building the person. The realm of the mind, unexamined thoughts—the Ego, in my perception.

Separation—rejecting that role defined Self. The realm of the Higher Self—calling—creating circumstance.

Liminality—a period of uncertainty. The realm of Higher Self vs. Ego, infinite possibility vs. limitations of comfort, heart vs. head.

Reintegration—working out "who I am" and becoming comfortable with that identity. Spirit shines through and manifests in our Higher Self expressed.

Individuation—fully accepting all aspects of self—the desirable and the undesirable character traits. Soul—neither "good" nor "bad" but complete and "real."

Our dreams and desires often keep us sane through the turbulence of an uncertain world. But what if we get what we wish for? What if our desires rush right up to us? Are we ready to embrace them or are they mere displacement, allowing us to live with our mind induced limitations? Our Higher Self is always leading us through our true heart's desires to our fullest potential. And what is our fullest potential but complete freedom to be exactly who we are, and to love ourselves as we are? Our Highest Self brings us face to face with our limitations. Limitations that are of the mind; many times unexamined memories before a time of discernment of what is actually true about us. Our heart's desires are of our personal truth and potential. When we break through and are anchored in our own heart, haven't we come home? And isn't that the safest place to be?

I think I will broaden my search for a place of transition. How about: East to the South of France, or Greece (they do have trees), West to California, and South to Costa Rica…or beyond? Why not?

The Midas Touch

The collateral damage of greed.

And so the king was granted his wish and whatever he touched turned to gold. He ran through the palace with joyful purpose—touching this and presto! Touching that and bingo bongo! Into the garden he raced and reached for a rose. Shazaam! The most exquisite gilded beauty… and then he put it to his nose. Oh. No scent. Too bad. So sad. Oh well.

Seeing his beloved daughter in the garden by the fountain, he reached out to kiss the soft blonde curls on her forehead. And lo! There before him a fearsome monument to his own avarice. Forever. No undoing it. No changing his mind. No rethinking the consequences. Once and for all time his daughter was lost to him. Her beauty, her innocence, her laughter, her love, her warmth, her glow, her breath—her life.

Would that she died and could have been buried, the king might have grieved her as lost through a nasty accident; a trick of fate. But no. She was to remain ever before his eyes. Still. Golden. Not dead, but not alive. How terrible to live with the consequence of one's aberrant choice. Too late to correct or repair—time only for remorse, regret, recrimination. A lifetime of hell.

And what is it to know that we have created our own hell? To know that our actions have not just killed, but have maimed, suffocated, spoiled and decimated all that is beautiful and life giving? And what is an aberrant choice? It is a choice that is anti life. It is a choice that is ignorant of the fact that the balance of life rests on a bee or a pelican—a krill. It is a choice that, to paraphrase Oscar Wilde, is based on the price of everything, but the value of nothing.

As a culture, we have become inured to the suffering around us. World Vision competes with Save the Children and we use our media technology to suffer the little children into our living rooms. Their teary, infected eyes crusted with flies laying eggs. Picking food from the dust. A tiny child caring for a tinier child, orphaned by war or AIDS or some such man-made disaster. The tragedy. The Pathos. We choke up—after all, we have kids—we're not the monsters, and we get out our credit card.

We mutter about the "brown" neighborhoods and are slightly distrusting of the communities that grow around the mosque. We are we and they are they and they don't understand "our" sophisticated society and choose not to blend. And if they are so different, can the terrorist "blood" not be pulsing through some veins? Do we pause to think why they might be here? Is it just to take advantage of our luxe—cash-rich culture, to rip off our government benefits?

Or might more of the cases be that they desired peace and sanctuary from a home country that is itself gripped in terror? A country where each child has a story of someone he knew and loved who was blasted off the planet before his eyes. Where the noise of nighttime traffic is missiles and tanks. Where the remote doesn't ever turn off the violence. Talk about degrees of separation. How far are you away from someone with no arms from a mine? Is there a whole generation of your family born with AIDS? Do you wonder if the water you sip for daily survival is teeming with cholera?

And now, "they"—big businesses, corporate (name your country)—have drilled a hole into the face of this earth—our very mother of nurturance and survival—and released a grim, black tide. Deepwater Horizon. What is that? A title? Will there be *Deepwater Horizon II*, the sequel? If we name it something pretty or exotic or grand will it be less terrible—more media-friendly, more culturally digestible? The image of the 'fondue' pelican has circled the planet at lightening speed – shocking and saddening us. There on the Internet. There on the TV. Those bastards! But wait.

Do you drive a car? Buy imported coffee? How do your heat/air-condition your home? I think nothing of hopping into my car and driving twenty miles at 110 clicks into "the big smoke" for a hair appointment. Then do it again tomorrow for a lunch meeting. I love Starbucks. I buy imported organic coffee at my local store here in King City. I have no idea how far it traveled to get here. I monitor the temperature in my home—but, hey—who wants to sweat at night? I thought of putting solar panels on my roof to heat the pool, but never quite got round to it. So…who is to blame?

It is no one and everyone. If our hungry maw of consumption squawked for alternate forms of energy, there would be no market for oil. Period. And the "bastards" would scramble for another way of making money that just might be a bit more conscious (because we would demand by our purchasing power that it would be so).

If we stopped for moment and turned down the volume of *Cribs* or *Lifestyles of the Rich and Famous*, we might, as a culture, begin to see that money does not equate superiority. Power, perhaps, but only if we give it over freely. Do the rich give us something we want? Sensationalism in entertainment? Genetically modified, neatly packaged, convenient microwavable food? Cars—sex or status magnets—that change with the season? A McMansion with Scarlett O'Hara staircase cheek by jowl in the community, that just a short while ago was a field that produced crops? Or is it oil we crave?

Who are the avaricious power mongering unconscious rich, and how did they get that way? In my mind, rich is to wealth what glamor is to beauty. One is of the world and the other of the soul. One distracts us and the other nourishes us. There is nothing wrong or negative about money. We should all have plenty. Money will feed the world—every one. Money will clean the water—every drop. Money will provide nourishing, untainted food for vitality and health. Money will support art and music and loveliness. Money is a medium of exchange. A very powerful one. But in and of itself, it is nothing but paper and metal.

Even gold—being hoarded by some and driving the price to astronomical heights—is of no value at all if it cannot be exchanged for clean water… because there is none. What good is a handful of gold if there is no bread because "we" have genetically modified our fields to their very death? What good is gold if a father can't kiss the tender rosebud lips of his child?

There is a price for everything. We live in a universe of balance. If that side goes up, this side will go down. Ipso facto. What is it you really, really want and are you willing to pay the price? Have you stopped to think what the price might actually be in the long run? For all of time there have been tales of deals with the devil. And who is the devil but the one who gives us exactly what we wished for?

I don't believe in intrinsic good or evil. Those values are merely opposite sides to the same coin. The yin and yang of perfect balance. The universal law. I do, however, believe that in our collective unconsciousness we as a cohesive interdependent mass of humanity have made a series of unfortunate choices that have put the planet in a precarious state.

Think about that and create this day by the Golden Rule.

Surrendering to What Is

How to experience life as an endless act of love.

Taking the hand of "What Is" is to engage in the dance of life. Sometimes we join in gladness and sometimes we join in sadness, but when we lean into the arms of surrender we experience life as an endless act of love.

This morning—four years ago—I looked into my husband's eyes for the last time. It was a magical moment of grace, free of fear or sadness. It began with the absolute knowing. In that clarity, there became nothing to do but to follow the lead of the moment. The handful of moments from first waking to last breath became a ritual of sorts. I had slept in a chair by the bed where he could easily see me when he opened his eyes. George had awoken fitful and perspiring.

I fetched the nurse to hurry up his meds and grabbed a fresh gown from the rack in the hall. To calm him, I filled a basin with warm water scented with lavender oil, and began to bathe him; his face, his hands, legs, feet. The nurse helped me put on a fresh gown. Waiting for the clock to strike 7:00AM and the pain relief to arrive, I performed Therapeutic Touch to offer whatever relief or comfort I could. I knew he was slipping away quickly, and by the time I had finished the treatment, he was gone. I climbed into the bed and fit my body into the familiar contour of his back, and held him. He was without pain and I was at peace.

I recount this not to be maudlin or dramatic, but because it was that peace—beyond understanding—that would define my life from that moment on. In succumbing to my own powerlessness I gained the greatest power of all. The power to transcend my own mind.

There were many life-altering lessons through the years leading to the morning of February 2, 2007. Each had the central pivot of death. On one occasion, I was reading a piece to my son and he listened closely before finally commenting, "Mom, people read your blog to be uplifted, not to read about death. Can't you write anything that *doesn't* include your pain and suffering?"

I didn't see it as pain and suffering. That would be whining. I explained that the whole context of my learning was pivotal from that experience and to write without hinging all to the experiential depth, I couldn't adequately give weight to the points I was attempting to make. While his comment wasn't the advice I sought, I took it to heart. I realized he was right about one thing and I was wrong about another. This I didn't realize until this morning.

My son was right about people not really wanting to hear about death. And while I wasn't writing from the vantage of pain and suffering, it must have seemed that way. What I was wrong about didn't occur to me until just now. It wasn't George's death that was pivotal, but instead my surrender to the inevitable. In that surrender, or humility, to accept the forces of nature as they played out, I was able to act in concert with the flow—and ebb—of Life itself.

The notion of "surrender" is a little misleading and this is where ego-mind comes in. We *think* we choose. We *think* we drive the course of the world. We *think* we can visualize and make it so. We imagine ourselves co-creators in a world that has been rolling itself out in evolution from the beginning of time. We *think* if we rail against the painful or difficult moments in our lives, we might somehow manipulate them or avoid them altogether. When we stop *thinking* and start surrendering or accepting what is, we will stop shaking our fist at the thunderstorm and go get an umbrella.

When the conditions are lined up for a thunderstorm, a thunderstorm there will be. We live in a physical universe with underlying laws or forces that manage the fulfillment of every speck of dust and galaxy. When conditions of dander, dirt, and breeze align, there will be dust under the bed. When conditions of stress, virus, and a sneeze collide, a cold is imminent. When conditions are right an egg will be fertilized, a cyclone will form, someone will become wealthy…or lose everything. Birth, death, winter, summer, gain or loss are points on a timeless cycle of evolution. How we experience these points is of our choosing. *That* we will experience them is *not*.

If we were to put our shoulder to a steamroller and push back, we will suffer a sore shoulder. Pushing against a steamroller is bad for our health and seriously impedes our capacity for happy pursuits. Yet we do it all the time! We push against the unfolding events of our lives—personal and universal—and think our push alone will alter the outcome when all conditions are aligned for something other than our intention. We know we are pushing when we act in fear or anger. This is the ego acting out.

The ego isn't bad. It is just living in medieval times and believes it is the center of the universe and that all events orbit accordingly. In truth, the ego is merely the sum total of all the memories, perceptions and experiences—conscious and unconscious—peculiar to the individual. If the ego is the iPod that we download all experience into, then the mind is the speaker—the headphone—literally. And anyone waking at three in the morning knows there is quite a jumble in there: Should I set up online banking? Did Aunt Myrtle live at number thirty-two or number thirty-six? Should I wear a suit tomorrow?

Our minds are so busy making sense out of nonsense that we are often distracted from conditions unfolding around us and step out into a busy street. If a particular series of conditions align—then whammo! No wonder we are afraid. We jump at the sound of the horn, are shocked that we lost our job, angry that we gained weight, and fearful that we might get sick and die. We miss our opportunities to influence the set of conditions. But it is possible to look both ways, care for our bodies, and prepare for eventualities.

Sometimes we can participate in the conditions and sometimes we cannot. When we cannot change the course of events and *accept* that we cannot, we finally begin to live in grace. Grace isn't a divine sprinkling that allows us to stay dry in the rain. It is an act of the will to be aware that there are forces seen and unseen that affect our life experience. We are at once the microcosm and the macrocosm. The raindrop as it falls into the ocean.

George had two doctors. One told him he was going to die and one told him he was going to live. We lived clinging to the pendulum swinging between hope and despair. There was no time for what was really going on: The end days to our life together. In complete exhaustion in the middle of one night, with my mind carrying on its own crazy chase, I surrendered. I gave up and just asked to feel the peace that I might be okay with whatever happened. In that moment I realized that neither doctor actually *knew*. I realized that what was happening was between God and George. Conditions that started at his conception, the conception of all his ancestors—his very DNA alignment—were manifesting in a complexity beyond any understanding. Add to that the chemical environmental damage that killed both his brothers with mesothelioma caused by asbestos, to which George was also exposed in his young years. All would result in his eventual and inevitable release from the physical body.

I could accept it or reject it. I could be fearful. I could be angry. I could medicate myself. I could bathe in sorrow and self-pity. I could pinion myself on guilt or remorse. I could beg God for a reprieve. I could weep on my sons' shoulders. But I could not change it. I could only surrender to it. I could be present but only peripherally. I could ease the process for us both but not alter it. I could interact with love and tenderness.

It is in the surrendering that we know peace. Peace does not supersede grief. If anything, it allows the grief its fullness and release. In surrender, I can see the blessing of George's life entwined in mine and I can see the gift of his death. Life is huge and unutterably beautiful. It *includes* death, adversity, poetry, roses, stars, and the smile of a child.

Without the conditions that included George's death I could not have chosen surrender. I would not have experienced grace. I would not have found peace. I would not have learned that in accepting the awesome totality of Life I have a greater capacity for love and compassion than I could ever have believed. I would not have known the lightness of being that I know today.

What died with George that morning four years ago was my belief in my ego-mind as authority. My ego didn't die. It is the sum total of all my life experience; the seams that hold me together as Marilyn. It is the content of my life, not the context. The context for my life is the same as yours. All Life. We rise up on the surface of the ocean, catch the sunlight on the crest of our wave, and then recede again into all that is and ever will be. In the beginning and in the end—Love is all there is.

What If the Resurrection Never Happened?

Not seeing the forest for the trees.

What if the resurrection never happened? I mean, what if there was no Judas, no pieces of silver, no Pilate—no Crucifixion? What if Jesus worked it all out with hugs and left everyone in his wake feeling warm and bubbly, as he flashed the peace sign and repeated, "Love is all there is?"

My question is how can we despise Judas when he fulfilled the prophecy of a new age dawning and served the peaceful warrior up on silver? He had to betray Jesus in order for us to pay attention. It's not human nature to go looking to change the status quo. So we paid attention but in the convoluted journey from then to now, we have betrayed that gentle message of love and compassion and awakening, over and over and over again.

In this story, doctrine has chosen to see the Crucifixion as the seed of suffering. To denigrate the betrayer and be satisfied by his remorse and suicide; to despise the governing official who turned away from the light and washed his hands; to distrust an entire race who turned against one of their own that dared individualism.

We have chosen to turn away from a message, which illustrates that only Unconditional Love can lift us over the horrors that man perpetrates on his fellow man. Just another atrocity. How did we miss that? By objectifying the man, the lesson, the *point*. Jesus's whole ministry—the few pages upon which we have built a world religion—is based on stories, parables, and allegories. He said it was *like* this: The lily, the mustard seed. He didn't say it *was* this.

Thinking to allow an external Christ to suffer our sins for us and obviate all personal accountability to our own Christed or fully actualized-Self is as absurd as standing in the field with the lilies, and expecting to be magically and beautifully clothed! It isn't happening! If you don't want to be cold and naked, you have to clothe yourself, and make choices of what seeds you plant for the harvest you desire. And for the really big questions—the ones where you "surrender" to the highest power of creation—well, you may have to look into eyes you know well and see the betrayal.

Sometimes the eyes that betray us first are those looking back at us in the mirror. They are the ones that do not see our pure potential, our own beauty, and contribution to a loving world. Or maybe we see it and look away. To embrace it would be to change the status quo, to dare to be different. What is betrayed by ourselves, or others we trust, is our own divine nature. We splash cold water onto a face that fails to match the magazine covers, look around a bathroom that is in need of remodeling, check our emails, grab our cell and dash out the door for another onslaught of making sense of it all.

We spend little or no time at all on what makes our heart beat. Just as we look for our salvation outside of ourselves, we also look outside for love, excitement, and meaning. And we look outside ourselves for sadness, destruction, and brutality. The terrible things that happen to us—lost job, poor health, loss of a loved one, a car accident or betrayal—are perceived to have been inflicted on us by others. Do we rail against the "injustice" or do we peer into the light of a larger meaning? When "bad" things happen to us we are usually drop kicked out of our status quo. The routine of the expectation of others goes kablooey! While the fragments of a predicted life are suspended, we can pause and look between them to see how our life might be rearranged into a more sublime existence. As we gaze at chaos we get to see what shines through—what really matters.

A Life Changing Event (LCE) is an opportunity for transformation. It is clearly for the person in the epicenter, but to paraphrase Shakespeare, we are all merely players on the stage of life. If you find yourself in the midst of an LCE then it is as much about you as it is for the perceived central figure. Then again, you are always the central figure in your own life.

Before I go on, let me state something unequivocally: The whole point of life on Earth as conscious sentient beings is the destination to a state of Pure Love. Period. *Love is all there is.* The boat we float to get there is our own life and how we live it. We can hoist the sails of authenticity and ride the sparkling waters in bliss, barely mindful of what lurks beneath. Or we can bump and grind along on a raft of cardboard, always sensing danger and reaching out for saving. The choice is ours alone.

God, if I may use the term, in His/Her infinite Love spills a cornucopia of experiences for us to choose from. I like to personify God, but most often I refer to the power and energy of Love as big 'L' Life or big 'C' Creation. Can't argue with the Life Force really, can you? It's all divine and infinitely beautiful. Yes, there are spiders and six-inch millipedes, but living with the creative force offers up some very weird and wonderful expressions—all valid—because they exist.

Back to the boat. I find I'm sailing a little faster now. Beside me is another charming little craft with bright sail unfurled. Athan and I call to one another and laugh a lot. We know our destination but we have no idea where it is or how we will get there. We only know that, for now, we travel together, side by side, and we are willing to let events unfold. We have one hand on the rudder and one on the mainsail sheet so we can take advantage of the winds and avoid the rocks.

Life is not something to offer up to Heaven to fix or take over. Your life is full engagement with all the creative force and trust you can muster. Living an authentic life is not for sissies. Jesus seriously did not want to go on that cross. Imagine being willing to offer yourself as a bleeding spectacle of surrender to a Higher Love and then witnessing the misunderstanding and watching it stain the promise of Pure Love like black ink in clear water! Forgive them. Forgive me. Forgive you.

Living your own authentic life takes guts and will. Knowing and accepting that life is fraught with challenges that make us stronger, lighter, wiser is the prerequisite for finding the peace and love we all seek. If you examine your own life from the perspective of a crisis—LCE—you will see that it was not random. Much preceded it and much more proceeded from it. Love is all that matters.

Can we see beyond the fear of life-changing events? Can we see the glimmer of love shining through difficult times like stars in a night sky? When the dove of pure Love enters and rests in our hearts, we will surely be invited to the final initiation of surrender. What do we surrender? All the things that don't really matter; including Life and Death as we know it. Life is eternal. Love is all there is.

I wish you love and peace, grace and a gentle awakening on this beautiful, symbolic morning—whatever your faith.

Mother's Day

Every day is Mother's Day!

No chocolate chip pancakes with jellybeans in bed for me today. Nope. This evening I am assured of a very special menu: Homemade pasta with a sauce or stuffing (not sure which, but I know it will be a culinary delight). I am to bring wine and a brick of Parmesan (my treat because the good stuff is beyond the budget of two young men forging their way in the music business).

Part of the pleasure of the evening with my two princes will be to watch them cook. They are a choreographed team in a small apartment kitchen. Today, the younger one will be in charge and the older one will act as sous chef. One will rinse a dish, and without turning his back, pass it over his shoulder where the other will scoop it up and put it in the dishwasher. What the…? I don't recall that at home!

They will finely chop, stir, and taste, rub a soupçon of spice between thumb and finger, and taste again. The candles will be lit, the table set with cloth napkins and mats. Stevie Ray Vaughan or another favorite will be providing the soundtrack to the festivities. Over dinner we'll watch a film that has been dubbed "for Mother's eyes"—so many aren't these days.

This last year I have learned the very biggest lesson about motherhood. It is this: If we want our children to do well in the world—and by that I mean be happy, productive, and develop loving relationships—we must see them for who they really are, and love and respect them for that. *And let them be.*

When I was seventeen, I handed my mother *The Prophet* by Kahlil Gibran, open to the page on children. My mother started to cry. I will quote parts here because it is, in my estimation, one of the most simple but pivotal treatises on parenting ever written:

> *Your children are not your children.*
> *They are the sons and daughters of Life's longing for itself.*
> *They come through you but not from you,*
> *And though they are with you*
> *yet they belong not to you.*

Today, as you celebrate Mother's Day, remember that at the moment of their birth, you literally laid down your life and allowed another soul to come forth. Whatever pain and suffering we might have endured in the moment evaporated as we gazed for the first time on that newborn face. We've been ecstatic and we've been frantic. We've been exhausted by their demands and we've rejoiced at their accomplishments. And ultimately we've learned more about our own strengths and weaknesses at the hands of our tiny teachers than we have taught them.

I have been buffed and honed into a more enlightened adult by witnessing my sons grow in confidence, accomplishment, sensibility, and awareness. The final polishing comes when we are willing to let go and trust in who they are. We really develop our personal strength when we can be witness in silence as their lives unfold. Jobs, education, relationships, talents, are just the brushes and paint with which any of us completes our own canvas as fulfilled human beings. We can offer perspective, but to think we know better is to grab the brush from their hand.

Their dad taught me: If you instill in a child self-love, they will never harm themselves or another. He also believed our parental role was to give our children roots and then to give them wings.

My sons are rock musicians and they look every bit the part. Long hair, earrings, be-ringed fingers, a wide brimmed hat with silver medallions. When flying they are "randomly selected" going through customs. They are cool. I'm a fairly straight and cultured looking dame and I must say the looks we get on the street when we walk arm in arm are quite amusing. They do cut a swath. Would I rather they were doctors or lawyers in suits more readily acceptable to the neighbors? Not if it was in exchange for their individuality and authenticity. It is only through being who they truly are and experiencing life on their own terms that they are prepared for whatever the future might hold.

This year since we all flew the nest of our family home to find ourselves, I have watched these fabulous kids become absolutely amazing and accomplished young men. As I've watched them develop in maturity, I have realized so clearly that an authentic, rich life is all about the journey and not the destination. They have attained a practical PhD in Life. I am not only proud of who they are, I also deeply admire them as individuals. I value their perspective on my life questions. I appreciate their confidence, honesty, and clarity.

I haven't been a brilliant mother. I've been overwhelmed. I've been uncertain. I've made good decisions and I've made…well let's call them decisions that taught me deeper lessons. But the other day, when I apologized to my youngest for not being as wise at a time that I might have been, he lovingly replied, "Mom, if you knew then what you know now, you would have acted differently, that's all." Wow, isn't that the truth!

When my son was a day old and being treated in an incubator for a slight case of jaundice, I went for a walk around the hall that encircled the hospital nursery. At the farthest point out, I heard my son cry. I hurried back as fast as my postpartum legs could carry me and went right to my babe's cot in the incubator. Sure enough, he was crying. It took only half a heartbeat to realize that I had never heard my son cry before, but had somehow recognized his voice—even at a distance. To me this was a stark realization that every human relationship is unique.

A child really and truly is Life's longing for itself. And as we all grow from child to adult we grow in the light of One who knows us. We grow into mastery of our own unique voice.

I think along with the bottle of red wine, I'll grab a glass of champagne to celebrate a Mother's greatest gift: Her child's self-actualization.

Pale Pink Cashmere Mind
1 of 3

Peace is the most luxurious garment.

When I was a teenager, there was an army greatcoat that hung on a hook behind the heavy wooden door in the cottage. On rainy days I would shrug into it, wrap it round me, and cinch the wide belt. It was khaki-colored with epaulettes. A real "trench" coat from the war when my dad was overseas. It was full of deep pockets and folds, and unexpected inner stashes. I would grab his old wide brimmed fedora, stained yet much loved, and pull it down over my eyes. Slipping into black rubber boots with the red trim around the top and toe, I would leave the cocoon of the fire-warmed cottage and slam the door behind me.

I would have to bang the door shut because the ancient wrought iron latch stuck sometimes before clattering into its slot and securing the door. The screen door would likewise bang shut in a twanging exclamation mark.

I loved walking in the rain at the cottage. The enormous pink granite hill on which the cottage perched would glisten deep red with undulating veins of clear white quartz. Oak trees flanked the rock on either side down to the road. At the end of our driveway, the gravel road curved this way to the left and that way to the right so that for the moment of decision, the way of the walk was unclear. To the right was the neighbor's farm, to the left meant I would likely walk without interruption and could even climb over upturned tree roots to clamber over rocks and into hidden pastures full of wildflowers and silent cows.

Before the adventure across the rocks, I would hit my stride. Long leading strides that stretched my legs and straightened my spine. Overhead, giant oaks and maples met and twined branches. In the spring, young frogs would sing from the ditches and in the fall, startling shades of red, orange, and golden yellow would lift my heart as they clustered in a matted tapestry along the gravel shoulder.

I loved that coat. It was like walking inside a tent. I was warm and dry and invincible. I would have gone walking either for escape or inspiration. Either way, I would be working something out. Thinking. Thinking. Thinking. The drops would fall and tap, tap, tap on the brim of the felt hat. The rain would be a damp presence on my shoulders. Into the woods on either side, the mist would rise and create a hushed and mysterious enclosure.

As I write, the scents rise up in my memory. Damp earth, pungent moss, dead leaves, fresh rain, a musty coat, wet felt. Interesting to think that our sense of smell is the only sense that we cannot avoid. While we breathe, we smell and since our recollection for over 10,000 differentiated scents far exceeds our image memory, I am reminded why I began this essay.

Yes....the pale pink cashmere mind. An army trench coat has stains and scars and deep pockets and unexpected folds. It holds things. It protects. It is heavy and gets heavier the farther I walk. This is our thinking mind. It holds things. It pretends to protect. And it becomes weighted with the detritus of memory—accurate and inaccurate, information—useful and meaningless. Our mind is a recording device. Like our noses, our open eyes take in all information. If I could access it, I could recall each and every tree in those misty, rain soaked woods that deeply flanked the dirt road. But, as the mind functions, I filtered out all that was not of "significance" to my thinking process of that moment. I walked my story, editing as I went along.

We get accustomed to the weight of our minds and forget that we can hang it on a hook behind a heavy door every once in a while. It is an exercise that begins with the awareness that we are encumbered by our own thoughts and thinking. I love the word "mentation". It is mental activity. Like a cow chewing its cud, and the constant din of city traffic. It is the noise of busyness. Think, think, think. Busy. Busy. Busy. Important. Exhausting. Distracting. Once we know that behind the noise and all the distractions, lies peace and tranquility, we can choose to use the mind rather than have it using us.

I realize separating mind from us in a *me* versus *it* relationship is to deny the integrity of body, mind, and soul of the holistic nature of being human. However, I don't know if it is by culture or by habit that we allow this mind of ours to become captain of our ship, when it is equipped, at best, to be first mate, or even cabin steward, fetching our stuff—memories and knowledge—and making us comfortable; providing context and wisdom.

When should we take off our mind and let it fall in a heap on the floor? How do we reach out and draw the soft pink cashmere sensibility into consciousness? The "when" is at times of intimacy, times of creativity, and those illuminated times of self-acknowledgment. Because we are inextricably body, mind, and spirit, the quickest route to consciousness is through the body. With the worthy and exacting guidance of the senses, we can slip out of the heaviness of mind and drift on the soft whisperings of direct sensorial experience.

Intimacy—true intimacy with another being—is too often tripped over and a precious moment passes in a blur of other thoughts. We have little blue pills to ensure human connection, but this is not intimacy. If anything, it merely distracts the mind with something more imminently important…for the moment. Intimacy is to release the mind altogether and is so much more than sexual. Intimacy is to allow ourselves to open to feelings of love, gestures of tenderness, acts of attentiveness. It can be a moment that we release ourselves, and like a drop of ink in water, in that moment our life is suffused with euphoria.

It might be the feather-light stroke of a lover's fingers that raises the hairs and calms the mind. It might be the scent of your baby's skin that closes your eyes in witness to miracles. It might be the vacant eyes of an elderly parent or friend that light up at the sound of your voice. It's the velvet of your cat's fur as she snuggles next to you and begins to purr at your stroking. It's the feel of the sun on your face sparkling through the yellow green buds of spring. It's the smell of lilacs, roses, chocolate chip cookies, pine forests, a loved one's shirt.

If we take the signal of our senses and pause we can release the weight of the mind. Go into that moment. Be there. Feel the touch; let the sensations transcend the mind. Pause; look into the eyes of your loved one as you embrace. Step into a warm tub and for that moment as your body eases beneath the water, experience the response of your skin in that stimulus. Allow sensation to fill your awareness. Sensation brings heightened awareness, and heightened awareness brings us into the feeling reality of our human being-ness.

Creativity—being the vessel of creation, the brush, the melody, the womb of new possibilities releases us from all judgment of who we are and are not. We drop the weight of the thinking mind and become the hands, eyes, voice of ever-evolving creation. We are authentic, at one with ourselves and always exactly as we should be—no matter whether our external experience is rain or shine. When we are in tune with Creation, we access unlimited potential for our unique personal expression in this world. Creativity is not relegated to the arts as we know them and to be sure much that we categorize culturally as art has no basis in creativity. Living a creative life is to see all that might be expressed through you in any given activity. It brings a vitality to even the mundane tasks of living.

Self-Acknowledgement—looking into our own eyes in a mirror or into our own souls through the reflection of silence, and saying, "Oh *that's* who I am." I am not the sum total of all that I carry as memory or experience. I am fresh and renewed every waking and sleeping moment. I endorse myself as I am now. This is my moment. This is my reality. I owe nothing and I expect nothing. I give all that I might and receive all that I need. There is no storm or turbulence that does not bring clarity of a new perspective. There is no opinion of me greater that the one I have of myself. What another thinks of me is their business, not mine. There is no circumstance that does not offer choice. The choice is mine to make.

My story is my story. Terms like dysfunction, rage, and blame are shoved deep into the pockets of a heavy mind. Anger, resentment, entitlement, and arrogance weight the shoulders of an unexamined life. Intolerance, manipulation, and coercion wrap in folds around our knees and trip us up. Your story is your story. It is not you—so drop it. Hang it up. Close the door on the storm of memory. It doesn't protect you.

Draw intimacy around your shoulders, inhale creativity with every breath, and embrace the most luminous Self you can be.

In the pale pink cashmere of my own beautiful life, I rest in elegance and beauty and wrap myself in the comfort of peace.

The Shame of Happiness

It's impolite to say you are truly happy.

I was raised to be "good." Good meant humble, passive, helpful, respectful, and self-effacing. I grew up "good" very well. So well, in fact, that Life scared me to death. Anyone older, richer, more educated, socially superior or just louder was awarded my abeyance and deference. Life in our turbulent family constellation was fraught with its dramas and tragedies like manic depression and suicide, and trussed up in the bonds of God's will. So God being the ultimate authority was good and scary and for sure ruled a world of sadness and uncertainty. Suffering was inevitable and enduring suffering without complaint was nobility itself.

But like every good Christian, I hoisted my burden—my imperfect Self—and set out to make that truth true. I looked for the broken people to whom I could relate. We shared a distrust of the world and the acceptance of a dysfunctional universe. It took me a few decades to discover that "thoughts become things" (in the words of Mike Dooley[4]), and I found exactly what I was looking for. Suffering. This "proof" fed my belief in my own unworthiness and even when—or especially when—someone saw me differently, as lovely or intelligent or worthy, I was quick by word or deed to prove them wrong…lest I be considered too sure of myself.

---

4 *Choose Them Wisely: Thoughts Become Things!* Mike Dooley, Atria Books

Then one day I met someone whose inner light beamed in a smile of such self-assurance, charm, and innate humility that I saw a crack in my reality and another world shining beyond. Like filings to a magnet, my disparate pieces of Self shot forward and gathered in the heart of this man. He became my new truth, my new reality. He spoke to me in my brokenness and said, "I will speak to you like I do my own daughters; if you have self-love and self-respect you will never harm yourself or another." This man became my husband and the father of two sons. He was my strength and my refuge. He was the mountain in the protection of which I made my home.

I grew in worldliness, accomplishment, competence, and confidence. I was happy. In his eyes I was best of all his desires. Imagine. If he thought I was terrific, well, it must be true. But then he died. He left me provided for—protected—with home and family and stature. But as wave after wave of grief rolled over the headland of my life and receded, I was left as an empty beach covered with disparate bits of myself. But then I discovered half buried in the sand, the treasure—the one he wanted me most to have but could not fully receive until he was gone.

It was the small pearl of self-love. And here's the thing: We are born with it. It is the flame of our own divinity. Want another word for divinity? I do. Let's call it *the spark from the brilliant flame of all that has ever been created and all that may ever be created.* As a definition, it's a little cumbersome, but it states it more accurately. Divinity denotes a more subjective realm as in, "Your God or my God?" Who can mess with the flame of all creation? Who can deem a spark of brilliance (sometimes hidden from itself) as unworthy or bad or wrong?

I was talking to my son the other night, and I commented how I admired his steadfast confidence in himself and his creative work *and* his profound and innate humility. His response was truly enlightening for me. He said, without pausing to think, "I think you can only *be* humble if you are confident in your own value." I asked him to repeat that, and he clarified by saying, "If you know your own value, you have nothing to gain by lording it over another. Humility without knowing your value is self-destructive waste." Wow, that hit home.

My learning was that to speak out about our successes and accomplishments was to be boastful and arrogant. To be humble was to truly hide your light. I got that lesson in spades. I also learned that to be worthy I had to be liked, and to be liked, I couldn't afford to be different. It meant the opinion of others counted more than my own.

Well, there I was back then on the beach holding the gleaming pearl of my own beautiful soul—the one un-encrusted by the hardened shell of a life of sadness and tragedy. But wait, I was knee-deep in tragedy. Happiness was the fleeting moment when the din of pots banging stopped for a second of blissful silence. Happiness is when you're not getting cheated or abused or frustrated. Or is it?

Happiness—true sustaining happiness—is a state of being that can hold all of life within it. Happiness is not the absence of conflict, anger, uncertainty, tragedy or sadness. Happiness is not the avoidance of some of life's colors: It is all of life's colors in tapestry.

The other day a young man told me, "You have no idea how dysfunctional my family is!" I was so tempted to say, "Oh yeah? Try my family's suicide quota on for size!" For those who remember Johnny Carson's stand-up shtick, at some point during the course of his monologue he would say, "It [the economy or some such] is so *bad...*" and the audience would chorus, "HOW. BAD. *IS*. IT?" Our tendency is to commiserate. But this kid was in the pain of dislocation from his own self-love, so that he would have to win the "how bad" debate to feel acknowledged and understood. There is no bottom to that pit.

Anyway, back on the beach I made a choice. I chose to be happy. I chose to acknowledge my story, and then drop it. Every day I have to actively choose to either allow my history to dominate me and end up feeling used, abused and righteously aggrieved, or to be happy. And now I am going to confess something in a way that flies in the face of all my "breeding." I am *happy*. Laugh-out-loud happy.

I have a fantastic relationship with my two sons. I respect them and admire them as amazing individuals. I have a rapturous, loving relationship with a partner who challenges me as we laugh at our folly of growing up while staying young. I have friends who are gifted and whole, and with whom I can share my successes as well as my setbacks.

I have my own business doing what I love. For a long, long time it didn't make money, but it was rewarding in its growth and taught me to hone my business skills. Now it's starting to pay its own way. What a novelty! What fun! I am happier!

I live in a great apartment in the heart of the city, which is very cool and very fun. Just this morning laughter and tinkling bicycle bells drew me to the window in time to see a hundred naked cyclists whizzing by along the street beneath! Does it get funnier than this?

In the previous chapter I mentioned my pale pink cashmere life of beauty and elegance. I am not describing my physical life. My actual surroundings reflect what pleases me—relaxed, untidy, bright and colorful. Beauty and elegance are states of being. And so is happiness. I am happy—not in spite of my tragic life but because of it. Happiness does not come bobbing in an open window like a drifting balloon. It rarely comes easily, except the transitory variety. True happiness comes in on the wings of Love. Self-Love first, then all that emanates *ever after* from that central brilliant and unique flame. You are the very source of your own happiness! Be proud of happiness. You deserve it and so do I.

The Myth of Happiness

"And they lived happily ever after."

I don't know about you but some of my happiest times have been after I have vanquished a foe—either in real life or in my beliefs; when I finally defined the lines of my personal kingdom and shoved someone or some thought into the moat. But here's the rub. All those nefarious creatures that engage you in thought, dream or reality, all reside within the walls of your kingdom. They infiltrated before you knew you were royal. Before you discovered the only one who can defend your walls is your Self.

And who are they? They are your parents. Their beliefs about themselves are seen through you. They are the cultural and religious mores and doctrines of your time. They are the collective beliefs of nation or global village. And who are you? *You are the spark from the brilliant flame of all that has ever been created and all that may ever be created.* Your preciousness is not debatable. Your potential as the hands, eyes, voice of creation is limitless. Your value as a human being is beyond all imagined riches.

This is the hidden treasure within the walls of your personal castle. You probably don't feel like the best thing that ever happened to the planet. You probably think you're screwing something up right now; your job, your kids' lives, your dreams.

My mother used to get so depressed and blame it on being a perfectionist. In my infinite insensitivity I laughed—you know, the big "Hah! *YOU* a perfectionist? *Look* at this place!" But now I know clearly that she *was* a perfectionist. She just never, ever measured up to the picture of perfection that was planted deep within her soul. Once you attain perfection then you will be happy. And she wasn't happy, so there was the proof that she wasn't perfect either.

When my mother was pregnant with me she went into depression. She was forty and a Baptist. Having sex for pleasure was frowned upon and certainly she wasn't planning a pregnancy at forty, so it was either pure, unsanctioned pleasure or my dad was a beast. So they got "caught out" and there I was. Proof of this nasty little business of making love. My mother went in and out of hospital for depression and finally, when I was three, one Sunday evening she left for a five-year period of treatment and rehabilitation.

Being a mother myself, and making a close study of the nature of bonding between mother and child, I know that the first notion of self-esteem and self-love comes from the gaze into your mother's eyes as you nuzzle at her breast. I can only imagine her tears of regret, shame, and confusion that overlaid the instinctive love I'm sure she felt for me. I guess I got the message, because for the next five decades, no material wealth, social status, devotion of another, professional accomplishment—not even great shoes—gave me the assurance of my own self-worth. My mother's message to me was always that she loved me "in spite" of me. I was never exactly sure what she meant by that except that I felt the source of great sadness.

Of course, no one would know it from the outside. My castle was beautiful with banners flying. Happy marriage; lovely children. But down, down, down in the dungeon of unexamined beliefs roamed the creatures of my own unhappiness. They were fear and doubt, recrimination and judgment. Anxiety was my default setting. I was waiting for something terrible to go wrong. Why? *Because I didn't deserve to be happy*. I didn't deserve to be loved by someone so wonderful. Being outwardly happy was a sure fire temptation to the fates or to God to knock you off your pillar. So I waited. Everything lovely tainted by a vague pall of foreboding.

And then of course it came. The rock on which my castle was built crumbled into the ocean of death and eternity. Interesting times—not only was the dungeon with all its demons broken open into the light, but there, resting in all the muck, was my tiny pearl of self love.

Happiness, I discovered, is within us—just as our demons are. True, lasting, unshakeable happiness is not the "tra la la." skipping down the leafy lane without a care type. There is nothing carefree about real happiness. The happiness we all seek but rarely find is not for the faint of heart. It begins with the most intimate care for your Self. That pearl of self-love needs rescuing and polishing, and only you can do it. But it takes the courage of a knight in shining armor to face the devils of doubt and fear.

Just as I looked for someone outside myself to make me happy, I looked for someone outside myself to fight my inner doubts. It was in the darkest days of my husband's illness when I was exhausted by terror, that I asked to find a state of peace so that I wasn't continually cast on the rocks of despair or dragged into the soothing sea of hope. I was completely at the mercy of my own suffering. I wanted the bad things to go away: Cancer begone. I wanted my life back the way it was.

No matter what I begged for—what I was willing to trade—the truth was evident. The end was nigh and there was nothing I could do to change it. I could only change the way I lived it. That was my turning point. All the spiritual work, all the psychological work, all the healing processes that I had engaged in over the years were mere Band-Aids over the deepest wound of denial of my own self-worth.

In the years since then, I have had the opportunity to meet my demons—thank you very much. When I minimize a page on my computer screen and it "disappears" I am reminded that our demons miraculously re-appear in one guise or another just when you need them. And when do you need demons? When you are in danger of allowing the light of your own beautiful eternal Self to be dulled.

Happiness is knowing that you are beautiful and perfect just as you are now. Doubts and fears and blame and manipulation and recrimination need to be jettisoned before peace can flow in.

What is my response now to the fact that my mother was depressed when I was born? "Boo hoo." If you saw *Lion King* (and if you are a parent—or kid—you did), you will remember the Graveyard of Bones. It was dark and cloudy and very, very scary. When you have picked over the bones of your own story and taken the meat of the learning, nourishing yourself, then let the rest drop. When the "facts" of your story come up and all the reasons why you can't be happy because of this or that or him or her, step over those bones or kick them aside. Resist the pull to share in what is wrong with life.

Life isn't perfect except for all that goes wrong. Life is all that challenges us to champion our own inner spark of truth, beauty, and perfection. True compassion for the suffering of another is to witness the battle that the spirit of self-love is waging against whatever challenge faces them. Remind yourself and others that the only key to happiness is self-love, and that can only grow in strength and brilliance when the way is clear of fear and doubt. It is a solitary battle. No one can do it for you, and you cannot do it for another.

Then again, once you understand the nature of true happiness, you realize there need never be a battle at all. All you need to do is continue to polish and nurture your own luminous Self and that will grow and glow in intensity, absorbing and transforming all that does not magnify its brilliance. What doesn't serve you in circumstance or relationship merely falls away.

What is the myth of happiness? That, once attained, the drawbridge rises and secures you "ever after." True happiness is the microcosm and the macrocosm. The tiny pearl of self-love within your own personal kingdom. It is the whole of all creation in its infinite potential for loveliness.

Santorini Sunset at Oia

Witnessing the human desire for beauty.

This past week we have seen and experienced some spectacular views. We have taken hundreds of photos—each one capturing a daub of color of the rich visual tapestry that is Greece. Emerald and ultramarine of the sea, fuchsia and magenta of the bougainvillea that spills abundantly over whitewashed walls. Red rocks, blue doors, black sands.

But last evening we witnessed something more extraordinary that lifted my heart in a way I will try to explain. The Oia sunset.

If you picture a bass clef of sheet music with a cluster of dots in front rather than behind you would have a stylized image of the island of Santorini. Oia, pronounced 'ee-ya' is at the top as the upper curve drops and curls slightly inward, on the highest point of the island and is apparently the sunset capital of the world.

In the height of the searing sun, we arrived in Oia and followed a tall young man who hefted our bag on his shoulder. Knee-high walls of whitewashed plaster are all that separates the walker from the drop. All the while, you experience the breathtaking view of the caldera—the crater of the once erupted volcano. You really need to pay attention to where you step, but ah—the view was a magnet for the eyes.

The last few steps led us to a small terrace with terracotta pots of brilliant coral and ruby geraniums and aromatic basil. A small marine blue gate led us into a tiny, enclosed terrace where I now sit and write in the quiet and the morning shade. A little salamander is finding its way among the pots. We are in a cave house—literally carved into the side of the cliff. Red lava rock defines the door and tiny windows with deep blue frames and shutters. We barely skim under the door lintel and not even into the mini kitchen (yes, I made contact). Our mantra after that first, painful incident is to, "Watch your head!" Good to have had some sailing experience.

Once inside the ceilings are higher and rounded. Rooms lead one to the other; living into sleeping into bathing. The bathroom at the back of the cave is shaped like the big, round loaf of pumpernickel used for spinach dip. The back wall is entirely of tiny sky blue glass tiles that easily meander around the curves and wave up to create the base of the open shower. The only straight lines in the room form the small, boxlike alcove for soap. Black lava rock peeks out here and there in the smooth white plaster walls.

Deep within it is cool, even in the thirty degrees plus of noon. It is charming and quiet and private. There is the slight scent of earth—not dampness, for the place is immaculately clean, but pungent. However, my western sensibilities are somewhat rattled and I am not certain if I am claustrophobic, suffering vertigo, the heat is getting to me or I'm just sliding off my perch a little bit. It was too hot to climb the steps back up and along the hilltop and past the castle ruins to find the long zigzagging stairs down to the beach, which, we are told is, "Way down there, just around the corner of the cliff below."

The tiny dots of bathers slowly traversing this course are like ants to and from a picnic blanket. At one point a line of half a dozen donkeys with green saddle blankets are led down the steps, bells tinkling, to gather up those who have decided to ride back up rather than climb. We will head down there today, if the way is not too challenging, before the sun gets too hot.

But yesterday, in the midst of the beauty and experience, I was disappointed. Without any real rationale, Santorini has been a spiritual beacon for me for decades. I thought somehow I would recognize something or Santorini would recognize me and I would feel the familiar. But I didn't, at least not immediately. Everything here is so completely unfamiliar that I was cranky and I blamed my banged head and the heat, and flopped on the bed in the cool inner room.

Athan joined me and we lay together, holding hands and gazing up at the ceiling. We both felt slightly disoriented. Double wooden doors, dark blue, fore and aft, shut us into this silent place. The white vaulted room and smooth lines created interesting shapes of shades of graying white. We instantly fell into a deep sleep and awoke hours later, at last feeling more willing to become oriented.

It is still hours before sunset, yet as we take the steps up to the street, they are lined with people sitting in the shade of the meandering walls, cradling cameras and bottles of water. As we scan the terraced hills and houses that culminate at the castle ruins, we are astonished at the number of sunset-worshippers already clustered along the top of the walls, down the walkways, on various terraces, all watching the western horizon. Still the sun is high and will not touch the top of the water for nearly two hours. The fascination is contagious and as we explore the village a little, we are continually mindful of the changing color of light that signifies the dipping sun.

More and more gather, sitting on steps, leaning on walls waiting, like fans for a rock concert. Laughing, chattering, but not giving up their spot. We decide to view the sublime vista from an enhanced location and choose a restaurant within steps of our little house. The terrace faces directly west and we settle at a linen-covered table with a small cushioned banquette. A variety of traditional Greek dishes are brought—each enhanced by the inspired chef, the charming translated English description, and the lovely presentation. The first sip of a glass of red Santorini wine—grown with no irrigation—is at once tart and sweetly savory, and spills over the tongue in search of every taste bud.

We enjoy the flavors and each other, ever mindful of the descending sun. The sea is radiant with light that changes from brilliant white to pink as the sun begins to drop more rapidly. It is extraordinary. As if punctured on the hazy, purple peak of the distant island, color spills across the horizon. Cameras cannot catch its intensity; words cannot describe the hues. I am at a loss. Orange, coral, red, gold. Nope. Garnet, amethyst, carnelian, amber, ruby. Better, but only the eye can adequately describe this spectacle to the soul. The sun is a pulsing and shining disc that allows itself to be drawn from yellow white, to gold to orange to coral to blood orange and finally to slip with a silent last wink beneath the distant silhouette of aubergine-hued islands.

And what happens then? A cheer goes up so loud and the Sun God is applauded for an extraordinary show: Well done! Laughter and shouts and clapping reach out and fill the caldera in infectious appreciation of Nature with a capital N. For that moment, each and every one of us is in the rapport of reverence. In reverence for what? For God, Nature, the Sun? It doesn't really matter. We are human, we are gathered, we are surrounded by inexpressible beauty and that is crowned by a moment of indescribable perfection that radiates out on the surface of the sea, which in turn touches every corner of the globe.

In this moment what we all share in common is that we have laid down our business, our cares, our desires, our fears, our grievances, and our differences to applaud the sun reflecting its bronze light onto every face turned toward it. The world smiles at us as we smile at it.

As I sit on the rim of the caldera and see the volcano long since exploded mirrored in the vanished sun's fiery red that lingers for hours longer, I think that as monumentally fearsome as Nature can be, it is man who emanates the greatest threat to our peace. In this moment, however, my faith in people is restored as I witness the deepest human desire for beauty, which is the truest expression of love. Santorini, perhaps you are the heart's center.

After Santorini

On the lip of a volcano, I found my perspective.

The sunsets in Oia turned out to be such a magnetic pull. No matter our busy late afternoon schedule—beach in the heat near the clear and glorious tepid rolling waves or napping in the cool of our little cave, we would freshen up and set out to find a new vantage for the setting sun each evening. Alternately, we found rooftop cafés, a perch on the wall of the ancient steps to the beach, a seat on the low, smooth wall overlooking the cliff, or from the winding walkways, where we watched the final descent through the still spokes of a windmill.

Every evening we joined the throngs standing at the highest point of the caldera on the crumbling wall of the fortress ruins, spilling over walls onto rooftops, and packing the cafés that described their sunset view advantage. Camera ready, we would wait patiently for time to move and the sun to descend into its glory. Each day was the same but vastly different; my perception was rapidly changing. The Aegean picking up the sparkling rays as the sun's brilliance spilled in a silvery shimmer. The ultramarine sea disappearing into the distance touched the sky and, as the sun gently eased toward the horizon, the path of changing light would reach right to your feet if you happened to be standing at the edge of the sea.

As the panoply of roses, oranges, golds, and purples flowed from the bosom of the dying sun, a wind would rise up like a long and heaving sigh from the heavens, and the day would be done. And there I would be, pulling a light shawl around my shoulders and trying to capture my hair as it blew in a halo of windblown curls. This caress of the warm and playful wind was at times cheeky and intimate. It would lift skirts and grasp anything not pinioned. The whole experience was at once personal and cosmic.

I and the sea and the wind are of the earth. The sun is of the cosmos. It's not a leap to imagine a culture that worshipped the sun as a god. Goodness knows, I worship the sun on the beaches of the emerald and aqua Aegean, and the sun returns the love with golden skin, food, the sunset—life itself. As the sun sets, the waters cool and the warm earth draws the breeze onto itself. I personify the "playful" wind, but it is just physics. Quickly cooling water mass next to slow cooling land mass, blah blah blah.

Yes, we can explain it but do we understand it? And where do we fit into this picture? Do we merely observe it, comment on the lovely colors and then turn our back on the darkening sky to go find dinner? Is the sunset just a daily spectacle or does it have more to tell us? We have taken our photos and have moved away from the lingering burnished horizon, but I have become reflective. Here we are witnessing the daily spin toward eternity as we sit on the very edge of an active volcano. Interesting juxtaposition, isn't it?

Here, weighted in the left palm we have eternity as symbolized by the ever "setting" and "rising" sun and in the right palm we have the ephemeral—our own life, for instance. The volcano reflected in tranquil waters of the sheltered bowl of the crater reminds me that we do not know the event that will take our final breath away. We may be warned and we may not be. So what?

In seven days on Santorini, I have documented seven sunsets in photos. In reality I have documented a moment a day in seven days of my own life. Days I have exchanged. Days I have "spent." I am reminded of moments when, as a child, I laid on my stomach on the rich pile of the Axminster rug on the floor of our living room. Standing, the jewel tones of the carpet traced a most intricate and beautiful pattern. Ruby on sapphire and in the dining room the reverse—sapphire on ruby. These rugs fascinated me. However, lying on my stomach watching *The Three Stooges* with my brother, I would drop my face closer to the floor and capture the scent of wool and dog. I would see into the tufts of blue deftly knotted beside tufts of red or gold or green, and lose the pattern in the pile of clipped fibers.

Why do I remember this? Because looking into the sunset is like looking into the fibers of my own life. What is the warp and woof; what ties it together; what patterns am I missing because my nose is too close to the detail? Am I mindful of what is important and life sustaining, or am I letting days drift by because I look into my own future and misperceive eternity?

What, in fact, is my currency of exchange for the days that slip by, some noticed, some not? What am I doing that, like sunshine, is my gift to the world? What am I doing that makes a difference? Do I spend my days in activities to create busyness? And if I do, is it constructive and productive and creative, or is it just busy?

Do I spend my days worrying about how to create income? And if I do, what does it buy? What do I exchange each dollar for? Comfort? Beauty? Loveliness? Something sustaining—uplifting—or just for stuff I don't really need or want? And what happens to those dollars I exchange? Do they, in turn, go to life-giving enterprise or do they fall into the hands of those who think that money gives them power over man and creation equal to the sun itself? Do I even care where those dollars go after I am satisfied in my need or desire?

Do I spend my moments in worry, anger, fear, or judgment? Have I missed an opportunity for love and tenderness when I have acted out in any of the emotions that cloud the light of love? Have I misused my finite energy—years, months, days, moments in ways that disregard the passage of time? Have I missed the most precious and certain gift of all—the moment I am now in? Am I caught in regret for past events, or hope for future happenings—memories or dreams of what has been or what might be?

Do I contribute to the wellbeing of Earth? Do I place the health of the planet as high as my own—which is one and the same, given my dependence on clean water and pure air? Do I live my life as if it really counts and do I see every aspect of life on Earth as valuable and intrinsic as my own existence (whether I understand the point of mosquitoes or not)?

For seven days I watched the sun set. It didn't actually set, of course; we spun away from it as the part of the earth I stood on closed her eyes in darkness. Earth spins in infinity while the sea and the wind and I carry on. The sea and the wind are the blood and breath of the earth and will cease when the sun itself fails to shine, and Earth spins no more. I, then, stand like a tree upright and alive for the moment. Yes, for the moment. I am inextricably connected to the blood and the breath of the earth and in that, to every plant, animal, and mineral on the planet.

In the city, from my apartment, I will not see the sunset, just the golden glow in the windows of the glass high-rise buildings. But whether I stand in witness or not, this day, too, will end—and the earth will spin another day and night until we might see the sun again as it will "rise" in the eastern sky. Since my first breath, I have spent 23,077 days. For seven days I really looked at what I have let go by for thousands of days, and it has changed my perspective forever.

On Santorini as the sun "went down" all the people who gathered on the slopes, walls, ruins, and in the cafes, applauded the spectacle and cheered Nature for her radiant performance, and then turned away. Like the rays of the sun, each one of us is a radiant performer if only we stop long enough to know it.

The Meaning of Courage
1 of 3

I'd rather be liked.

When I first began to study the *Bhagavad Gita* with my spiritual teacher, she advised her small group of students, "Be aware that when you study the sacred scriptures, Life will offer you the circumstances to understand the lessons." That is certainly my experience. Choosing to live from a higher understanding frees us ultimately from pain, fear and suffering—but (and here's the catch)—not without experiencing it first.

It is in walking through the fire of fear, betrayal, loss, suffering, and grief that we see that this is the fire that strengthens the steel of our character and spiritual expression, and burns away all that does not serve the Higher Self.

I sent out a prayer request last week to my LightBeam Community because my world was rocked. It seemed that no matter what I did or said, the vortex of negative energies gathered in strength and I felt truly isolated and frightened. Of course it is at that precise moment of surrender that we have the opportunity for our greatest enlightenment. And if we are truly open to receiving that awareness of what conflict means to our soul's evolution, the light shines brightly and those whom we would call enemies of our ego-based human self are in fact the friends of our spirit-based Higher Self.

There is no sidestepping the experience of life on Earth. We are born and die, and in between we run smack up against the harshness of the physical and finite world. The Buddha said, "Life *is* suffering." But if we embrace that vital truth, we can detach from the sense of guilt of making mistakes, to the awareness that we do not need to be attached to these various events to learn from them. In fact, to be attached and engage in trying to prevent or "fix" something is to ensure our continued blindness and suffering.

Issues we face that challenge us to act in truth, conviction or courage are never about what they appear to be about. The world is a stage and that is true. It is the Earth Theatre upon which we act out our character parts. Someone enters stage left with a sword and we play out coward or champion. Each completed role portends the following acts and scenes. To live a happy life and die a serene death is to be exactly who you are until the final curtain call. Once a foil's part is played, we can allow him to exit and hold no further influence.

No matter what we are born into or what we grow through, we are unequivocally souls in evolution. Our every action is a choice to free ourselves from the bonds that keep us ensnared in the collective belief that Earth is all there is and what we do to one another doesn't matter.

The very reason my website *LightBeam* exists is my deepest desire to be part of the change for a world based on love, gratitude, happiness, collaboration, goodwill, vitality, beauty, creativity, and the prosperity to share all this. Those who read and follow my website, I trust, are like-minded. This is not the world that surrounds us right now. But it is my conviction that if we all act with integrity to these values, we will eventually live in that world.

> *"All that is necessary for the triumph*
> *of evil is that good men do nothing."*
> Edmund Burke

In the *Bhagavad Gita*, when Arjuna gazed upon the army he faced, he saw uncles and teachers and those who had been friends. He recoiled and appealed to Sri Krishna that it would be better for him to die than take the life of one he knows. "What is the honor in that?" he asks.

Sri Krishna explains that, as a warrior, it is his spiritual duty to fight evil. To turn away from one's duty is to incur sin, and as Burke says, allows evil to triumph. Krishna explains that since we are all souls, both victor and vanquished ultimately return to spirit. There is no avoiding the end for good behavior. So if I truly desire the world I described above, I must act with integrity to those values in all I do. And that means that sometimes I will be unpopular, challenged, and defeated by those who gather the forces of all that is not of that same light-based reality.

People will say I am a troublemaker. People will say that I am having a nervous breakdown. People will say that I am interfering with their "spiritual" relationships. And I say, I can stand in the clear light of my truth, but can they stand in the dark of their lies? What anyone believes and what happens next doesn't even matter. Circumstances have guided me into my strength and away from energies that do not serve me any longer.

Why, then, if I'm such a lofty spiritual being who is aware of the Big Picture over the Little Drama do I need to have prayers said for me? Because we all need a little help from our friends. Because the cosmic soul is seeking expression through each one of us and we must answer that yearning as best we can. And because the soul is using this body on this earth to stretch its boundaries and reach its highest expression. I am human. I weep when I am not loved. I am hurt when I am struck. I wince when I am attacked for just being who I am. When I lose someone I loved through death or other leave-taking, I grieve.

When I am challenged to face those I fear, it takes courage and fortitude. My body responds with every physical response as if I were on the battlefield. Adrenalin courses through my body, my heart pounds as though it would leap out of my chest. My whole nervous system is on high alert. I have felt a lance through my solar plexus. These are days when I want to pull the blankets over my head until the world gets sane again. But of course the world is insane. Sri Krishna said to Arjuna, "Get up, Arjuna, and fight!" And so, too, did I.

These days the battle is for truth. And sometimes just being still in our own quiet truth wages the battle. As I discovered, the battle came to me. I could have walked away, but as I said in my request for prayers, this was an epic battle between light and dark, and so was on the plane of the Big Picture. The challenge for me personally was to choose if I would stay enslaved to the "good" opinions of others or stand in my own light.

I hasten to add here that choosing to express the Higher Self is not an act of superiority—of good over bad. There is no such thing. When I use words like deceit, betrayal, toxic, I am describing as accurately as possible my emotions and my experience. These are not words of judgment. People acting in the Little Drama act consistently with their nature for the very survival of their psyche and their person. I have no doubt each felt justified in his or her actions. In fact, I hope they did because otherwise that would be just crazy. But just as the pearl needs the abrasion of sand to form, so the soul chooses conflict to grow.

There is only choice and experience and how those choices result in the life we desire. What is our overriding desire? To be liked and approved of? Or do we want to be accepted exactly as we are—with all our strengths and frailties?

So, coming back to my personal epic battle, which Joseph Campbell so brilliantly depicts in *The Hero's Journey*, I was challenged to stand my ground and speak my truth, and allow the maelstrom of opinion to swirl on in its destructive path. My pain and suffering stemmed from my desire to fight a bloodless battle. To fight for my Self and all that I stand for and still have everybody like me. My attachment to a pleasant well-sorted outcome was causing me anguish. Through prayer, meditation, the prayers of those who love me, and through spiritual texts, I was able to climb above the melee and see that I was free.

The demons I fought in these persons were the demons of my inner longing to belong. I had looked outside for my sense of worthiness and had to learn—painfully—that I am worthy to myself. Today, for the first time, I belong to myself. My heart is strong and I love who I am—all of me, as I am—a quirky work in progress.

Sympathy vs. Empathy

With a little help from my friends.

So many friends have written or called this week with kind words—sorry that I have been saddened or in pain, concerned that I am all right. I appreciate it because—believe me—in the midst of the drama no one feels sorrier for me than I do. However, the reason I am so explicit and exposed in my experience is not to kvetch or whine, but to share an experience as a map out of the tangle of the Little Drama and into the vast and beautiful landscape of our own Big Picture.

When I seek prayers—positive energy and love—it is not so others will weep with me, but so that with the collective outpouring of love through focus, whatever is needed will find its way to me, and to those with whom I am engaged in the drama. We are all gathered to learn something about ourselves and then to choose which road we will take into our respective futures. The choice is either to stay in the Little Drama of anger, resentment, judgment, victimization, and turmoil, or to see that the Big Picture beckons all souls to the peace and pleasure of being whole and at ease with their true nature.

Sympathy is dangerous because it is a bellows to the sparks of the parts of ourselves—our broken selves—who would stay hurt. In the *Bhagavad Gita*, Sri Krishna shares these famous words with Arjuna:

"The Self cannot be pierced by weapons or burned by fire; water cannot wet it, nor can the wind dry it. The Self cannot be pierced or burned, made wet or dry. It is everlasting and infinite, standing on the motionless foundations of eternity. The Self is un-manifested, beyond all thought, beyond all change. Knowing this you should not grieve."

Those who seek real freedom from a life of reaction to a life of pro-action and true co-creation within a beneficent universe, must be willing to heal from the inside out and release all attachment to any outcome other than the higher understanding of their Selfhood. We cannot avoid the difficult, the painful, the acting out of damaged people or life itself in its beginnings and endings. We are all damaged in one way or another, or we wouldn't keep recreating Little Dramas that keep us enslaved to a conflicted world.

When we come up against some demon in our life—someone who means us ill—we can be sure that this person is only activating a broken part within ourselves, which needs healing. It's the whole plot of *The Wizard of Oz*, the *Bhagavad Gita*, and innumerable other parables trying to guide us to self-actualization and mastery. No matter how painful and out of your control it may seem; the answer is how you embrace the opportunity for personal growth. Will you throw yourself on the floor and beat your feet and fists until someone comes to protect you? Or will you face your fear, anger, shame—feel it, interact with it, and release it?

Many healing modalities and energy based practices offer the individual access to the scripts and broken bits that keep us enslaved to deleterious relationships, habits, or practices that affect our health and our happiness. It's fairly easy to drop down into those dark corners, but what happens then—when the tears of rage or shame or sorrow rise up through the body in a cell or muscle memory? The wise practitioner will stay impartial. Will not reach out to soothe; will not attempt to distract the soul from the cleansing of its own emotional release. To do otherwise is to jam a sliver back into an infected finger.

I know it is counter-intuitive when someone we love appears to be suffering not to reach out and say, "There, there." But it is the truly loving and healing response to stay quiet, centered, and supportive while the little self breaks apart and the pearl of the Highest Self shines through.

On the day my darling husband was told he had only weeks to live, we had a lovely two martini lunch and spoke in quiet voices about the future. The future that day was two or three weeks hence. We were clear and strong and loving with each other. We held hands and rested our foreheads against one another's.

Then George went home and I went nuts. I was frantic. My pact with God—as I read it—wasn't panning out. And the one whose arms I would rush into and whose shoulder I would weep against was the one who needed to lean on me. I knew I had to share this grief and this terror with someone, but I knew intuitively that this was a monumental passage for my own enlightenment and whomever I sought for counsel was vitally important.

That very hour I called and went to the only one who I knew would understand my plight in its magnitude: The one who taught me about Arjuna and the teachings of Krishna. I arrived at my beloved teacher's house and after a quick embrace at the door she took me into the kitchen and made tea. Sitting near me, Gita held my gaze while I spilled over in tears of fear and rage. I wanted her to hold me. I wanted her to comfort me like a child and tell me everything would be all right. But she didn't. Everything wouldn't be all right. My life was about to change dramatically and would never again be the same.

What Gita knew was that I was not a child; I was a soul in training. She also knew that I would be walking a path of great challenge over the next weeks and months, and in order for me to transcend by this amazing opportunity for love, compassion, and acceptance, I would have to be more than strong. Strength in our language terms often means stoicism, denial, and diminution of real events. Strength in soul terms means awareness and understanding that is unshakeable against the storms of life.

The only way we plumb the depths of Life with our roots of love and understanding is to have the experiences that cause us to reach deep. Deeper than sympathy. Deeper yet into the inexhaustible pool of love to which every soul on Earth has access.

After I dried my tears that day with Gita, I went home. My surrender wasn't instant but rather than skim over the real events, I was completely engaged. It was a time when I gave up my ego self that could bargain with God or fix things. I surrendered to the fact that my darling husband was dying and that I was powerless to do anything but be a witness, and to minister to that inevitability with simple acts of love.

My latest drama this month, for which I asked for the power of prayer, was just another opportunity to peel off a layer of what was not serving my highest good. Yes, I got caught up in the pain and suffering. Within us all is the fearful child. The one afraid of being abandoned or not loved or not accepted. I asked for prayers because I know that I am not a child in need of solace, but a soul in the deepest yearning for freedom, peace, and happiness.

The world of the Little Drama is full of small-hearted people acting out behind a screen of power. Those of you reading this know that the only real power is the power of love. And when we claim that power for ourselves we are freed.

Lies Are Like Mice

Left unchecked, they cause a plague.

My sons live in a very cool apartment—1,600 square feet—huge with two bedrooms, high ceilings, and a big kitchen. It's a great address, if you are up and coming musicians. The only thing is it is over a restaurant, which is ideal if you like to party after hours, but not so good if you'd rather not deal with mice and various other such nefarious creatures from time to time…notwithstanding the landlord's claims to the contrary!

But mice are little and innocuous and kinda cute when they skitter as the lights go on. And if you've been raised to love nature in its wholeness, you naturally have an aversion to snapping their little necks in a trap set with cheese (or peanut butter for the more savvy).

My sons were loath to kill the little things, so I told them a story. Years ago when their dad and I lived on a farm in Port Hope, we faced a similar challenge. It was a magnificent stone house; one of five built by Scottish brothers who had immigrated in the late 1800s. One day we saw a little mouse sprint under the cupboards into the back pantry under the stairs. "Oh," I cried, "don't kill it!"

Not many weeks later, an unmistakable odor emanated from the pantry. No longer did the little darlings skitter when the lights came on. They had become bold and saucy and stared us down. That was it! We bought a dozen traps. This was our house after all—not theirs. What we soon discovered was that, when you regularly spot one or two brazenly out and about, there are likely ten or twelve lurking below decks. And being the bottom rung along with rabbits of the food chain, well, don't they just multiply like…rabbits.

I was squeamish but nevertheless, twelve traps were set in the pantry under the stairs one night before bedtime. We were kept awake with SNAP! SNAP! SNAPSNAPSNAP! For several days we had a virtual slaughter. We felt terrible for killing them, but eventually the odor subsided and our pantry was no longer the toilet of vermin, our rice wasn't intermixed with dark lookalikes, and we were once again at peace.

I share this story because lies are like mice. Especially the little ones. My dad used to say: "If someone will lie about the little things, then they will definitely lie about the big things." But somehow we don't live like we know that. We let little transgressions go by because we don't want people to think we don't trust them. We let them go by because we can't imagine that someone would lie to us. We let them go by because, well, why make a big deal of a small issue?

Why indeed? We know the little lies are there, breeding under the floorboards—but what the heck? We'll deal with it later. But history has taught us that unchecked breeding of vermin results in the plague—and isn't that exactly what we are witnessing on a global level? A plague that wipes out truth. A plague that wipes out trust. A plague that wipes out creativity and freedom. A plague that wipes out credit, homes, life savings. A plague of lies that is global and threatening and suffocating and frightening in its immensity.

And whom do we blame? You got it: THEM! *They* did it. *They* stole, *they* lied, *they* cheated; *they* were rich while we were poor. *They* were powerful while we were weak! But is that true…absolutely?

Look again. Then ask yourself, what is truth? What is honesty? What is the difference and why is it important?

There is only one truth, and that is your own. Shakespeare's Polonius said, "To thine own self be true." Aligning with our personal truth is aligning with our creator. Each of us is singular and unique. We are a composite of influences—body, mind, and spirit within the construct of family, environment, and society. Many of us, somewhere along the line didn't feel that being just who we are is good enough, so we discover the little lie: "I am not good enough."

The expectations or pronouncements of others obscure the spark of unconditional love and infinite possibility, which is our true nature, and we confuse the lie for the truth. In order to belong and be liked, or be rich or be powerful, we engage in this collective lie: "It's only a lie if we get caught."

Those of us who hear the whisper of truth through self-realization or lie-shattering experience snap out of it. And there we are, rubbing the veils from our eyes and seeing people around us for the first time. The first shock is seeing our own complicity. We have agreed to lie to one another: "I will accept your insincerity as long as you praise me." "I will overlook your actions against another as long so it is not against me." "When I see injustice, I will bow my head until it goes away."

Once you awaken though, you are no longer at liberty to be tied up in the collective lie. But—here's the kicker—you can't just turn your back on it either. The plague grows unchecked and spreads into the hearts and souls of us all if we don't stop and face it squarely, one lie at a time. First, check the lies you tell yourself. Then check the lies you allow those close to you to tell you. It will startle you when the masks fall. You will blush at the weave of agreements you made along the way.

Standing in your truth is not socially correct, by the way. It makes people feel uncomfortable. And sometimes you have to shout the truth to be heard over the gaggle of lies. We sometimes confuse the spiritual path with the path of inaction. But some of us—make that all of us—are called to be spiritual warriors at some time or another, whether we act on it or not. For me, the image of Archangel Michael with the sword of sapphire fire has my back.

The other little caveat that needs to be said clearly is that, like any rat cornered, the one whom you present with his or her own lies will attack. It is, after all, the struggle for survival. I never really understood Nietzsche's "will to power" until writing this piece. I guess I equated power with force and I never wanted to be an overlord. But what I unequivocally understand is that if we do not exert our power for what is beneficial, then those who act out of avaricious self-interest will exert their power to dominate.

You have no control over what others will say about you and you have no control over what people may believe about you. All you have is all you've ever done and stood for, and judgment upon that is most stringent by your own highest nature. There is no win or lose, good or bad, right or wrong. There is only you being true to yourself.

Our true survival past fear, past anger, past manipulation is through expressing our Highest Self. Each of us is a higher being and each of us has a choice about whether we express our light or our dark; our love or our pain. We are all free to act and if those of us who have awakened to this reality act in light, then those in the corner will have another opportunity for choice. If they choose to continue in the lie, they relegate themselves to the ways of the lie, which are spite, anger, and fear. This point is the most difficult for me not to slip into the drama—the lure is very strong to be the victim, the injured, the unloved. Sometimes you need to be reminded who you truly are to stay strong and clear.

The world you knew will probably topple and you will find yourself standing in the middle of a cloud of dust and a heap of rubble. I know I did. The fallout is seismic and affects everyone around you. If you agree with some of the precepts of energy medicine, then you will understand that a shift to truth, like falling dominoes, will not only affect this world but will reach forward and back through time and space, correcting patterns and dysfunctions for generations.

Why would anyone want to pull their familiar world down around their feet? Because the soul wants a clear view, and when the view is unobstructed, your vantage point is 360 degrees. Not only will you see, but you will also no longer be obscured from others who seek the truth. That is exhilarating but also scary in a way. In which direction do you step out into your future? Well, toward the truth.

And what is the overriding cosmic truth? *That love is all there is.* The corollary truth? *What we do to one we do to everyone.* If we lie to ourselves, we create a world of deceit. If we stay true to and love ourselves, we create a world of peace.

Love Like There is No Tomorrow

1 of 3

The truth about 12:21:12 or any other day.

There is a big truth about 2012 and there is a little truth about 2012 and they are both the same: **It Does Not Matter!**

The other day, I was chatting with an industrial psychologist. She goes into large working environments—in this case corporate or industrial—and assesses every person from plant sweeper to Chair. In-depth psychological analysis, combined with years of experience and intuitive skill, allows this professional to advise on the best way to bring each individual to his or her optimum level of potential within the business entity, for the greater good of the whole.

At any rate, she shared that a prevailing concern for many was the specter of December 21, 2012: "The end of the world." I was really surprised by that. I thought the whole Mayan Calendar thing was more in the realm of New Age and that the infiltration into popular consciousness was a one-off disaster film. But, it seems fear is a sticky thing and what for many of us is a call to awakening is for the masses another reason to fear the unknown and uncontrollable.

Fear is debilitating. It's also completely illusory. The popular anagram F-E-A-R spells: **F**uture **E**vents **A**ppearing **R**eal. Now, a future event hasn't happened and may not happen, and may unfold in infinite possibilities and combinations of probabilities—but there is that variable of the unknown that is unassailable. And in our minds, we can only hold in our imagination of the future what we already have experienced.

If we dream of a frightening end to the world, we can quickly reference trillions of recent films in full digital effect…or a daily dose of CNN. If we dream of a benevolent future, we can envision *Avatar* and lovely scenes of crystal palaces populated by abundant flowers and birds and loving folks, all caring about the beautiful Earth that sustains us.

But fear is like black velvet in a dog-grooming studio. It attracts everything! If we're not worried about the world banks or whole governments going bankrupt, we may be worrying about our jobs or our children. The other day I was rushing through the subway and saw a huge lit-up poster. Something unnerved me about the image, though it was just a little toddler standing on a beach looking out over the ocean. The next time I went by I read the caption: *This time next year, she will be diagnosed with cancer.*

I was outraged and heartsick at the same time. Media plays to our greatest fears. Day after day, minute after minute, we are assaulted by our worst fears and they are printed up and thrown into our face in glorious Technicolor—we are drawn in and then slapped down! Or the images are dire and horrific: Children with flies on their crusted eyes, icecaps melting, rivers on fire from pollution, rainforests—the lungs of our Earth—decimated. Most times, we soak up these images subliminally. They don't exactly register, but instead wriggle down into the shadow where our other unconscious fears reside. Like burrs, one sticks to another until the cluster is like a prickly straightjacket that robs our lives of joy and meaning.

What does this have to do with 2012 and the end of the world, and how could the end of the world not matter? Well, this: Your life—yes *yours*—the life of the one reading this—is going to end. It will end only one way: By you taking your last breath. Through your last exhale you will return to where all Life begins. When and how that will happen is only speculation. Will it be a world cataclysm, a group ascension, an earthquake, drowning, heart attack, car accident, or in your sleep? It doesn't matter. The result will be the same.

Many who are given a terminal prognosis of disease live to say how grateful they were in how it changed their lives; focused them on what was truly important, and allowed them to find joy in simple pleasures. How often have you heard of "miraculous" remissions or cures when a person's whole outlook and lifestyle have changed?

A death sentence provides an incredibly beneficial filter for what is worth spending time on and what isn't. Somehow we take the doctor's pronouncement as more authoritative than Life's itself. The fact of our birth *is* the fact of our death. Each breath we take is a breath of Life, each breath we exhale, is one closer to death. Instead of getting twisted into tangles about the unknowable end *then*, ask yourself *now*: What are you spending your time on? What are your predominant thoughts? Which relationships enrich you and which relationships tear you down? Where can you be compassionate and draw someone more closely *into* your life, and where can you show compassion for yourself and let someone go *from* your life?

If you really believed the world were going to end in a handful of days, how would you spend your last? Where would you like to be? Who would you like to have told you love them? What gifts of inspiration would you fulfill to know that you have expressed the unique soul you are? Death is a very personal and independent event. Even if we were to be annihilated in one swat, each of us would have our own singular experience.

When my husband and I finally "gave up hope" and came to terms with the inevitability and imminence of his death, which turned out to be only weeks away, I suggested we begin to prepare him for that passage. I also made a commitment to myself that day that I would begin to prepare for my own death. That may sound maudlin, but I assure you it is the most freeing perspective. The best way to prepare for our ultimate last breath is to live life to the fullest—every minute of every day!

Oh, how often we forget to remember and we race down a rabbit hole of grand schemes of false priorities. How often do we sacrifice to please or appease and leave ourselves distracted from what we do best? How often is the opinion of another more important than the opinion we have of ourselves? How often do we allow the burr of the thought that we are not good enough, smart enough, experienced enough, young enough or beautiful enough to hitch onto other burrs of similar thoughts?

If we could just remember that catching our last breath on Earth is on a countdown as strict as catching a flight, we would be a little better organized in what we did and didn't do on the way to the airport.

Just as Death is personal, Life is also very personal. In fact the only meaning it has is the meaning you give it. No one else—not your baby, lover, mother, boss, not even God can give your life meaning for you. No one can read a book for you or digest a meal for you. You are the one. The only one. The relationships and circumstances in our lives are tools for us to find and express that meaning. Let that meaning be worth dying for. Tomorrow or three hundred tomorrows or many thousands of tomorrows from today.

Rather than fearing an unknown and unknowable cataclysm of a debated prophesy, embrace what you do know and live—really live—in the freedom and joyful abandon of that inevitable moment when your time will be complete. Love *now*. Forgive *now*. Look after your body *now*. Be grateful for all you have *now*. Be tolerant *now*. Be kind *now*. Be gentle *now*. Be courageous *now*. Stand up for someone less able than you *now*. Stand up for what you believe in *now*.

And love some more. Love yourself *now*.

Love is like water. When it is poured it finds every space, fissure and cranny and fills it to overflowing. You cannot guide the path of water, water finds its own path – and so does love. When you pour love out of your deepest heart you stand in the center of the fountain of Life *itself*.

December 21, 2012? November 29, 2011? Or Stardate 41153.7— none of these dates matters in the scheme of your own Life fulfillment. This day is the one you are unequivocally alive. *Live* it that way. And love like there is no tomorrow!

Love the Earth Like a Mother

The big truth about 12:21:12 or other presumed apocalypse.

In my last chapter, I said there was a big truth and a little truth about 2012 and neither mattered. This piece is about the big truth—the truth about our planet and very mother of existence: Earth herself. And what doesn't matter about that?

Well, this: Earth is about five billion years old. In cosmic years that may be teens, or young adult, or even middle aged, but however you look at it, chances are she'll keep spinning through space long after December 21, 2012. Certainly well into "stardates." Whether we are having a happy ride on her back or not is quite another matter.

Last week, I had the pleasure of visiting the Mayan Exhibit and the Dinosaurs at the Royal Ontario Museum with my stepdaughter and her young children. There it was, all laid out—clear evidence of giant reptiles, eggs, and all. Downstairs there was equally clear evidence of a culture—civilized and elegant—buildings, jewelry, and art. And the common denominator is that both populations disappeared off the face of the planet and both extinctions remain steeped in mystery and speculation.

Our Earth nourishes every living being with oxygen, water, and food. Our ecosystem is balanced for plentitude and no waste. All natural systems cycle on birth, expansion, death, birth, expansion, death and on into the life cycle of the planet herself. The atmosphere today is more beneficial to humans than dinosaurs. Mother Nature gives birth and sustains all life—regardless of whether first life spawned from primordial ooze or sparked from the stars themselves.

The sun shines through a protective atmosphere with equanimity and warms all skins (irrespective of color), grows all plants (irrespective of genetic modification), lights all corners (irrespective of "good" or "evil"). Earth spins and the sun shines regardless of the folly of those of us running in fear of the end of the world.

Earth has shown us that while she can rock us in a cradle of infinite peace and beauty, she can—with a mere shrug—cast hundreds of thousands of creatures into their own eternity through an earthquake, volcano, tornado and/or other natural occurrence. She doesn't give much warning, and when she's done, continents have shifted and islands are born and Earth spins on into her own expansion and life.

In other words, the earth might wobble, but she will certainly out-spin our puny existence. Ice core drillings in the Antarctica have shown that over the past 450,000 years, the earth has gone through heating and cooling, melting and ice ages several times. The chances of the human race snuffing the earth by our own stupidity are slim. We are without a doubt in our mindlessness, an annoyance; but wind and water and the will to power of Life itself will overcome our silly schemes of domination over Nature.

Just look at a tiny seed growing through a crack in concrete and breaking it apart in its delicate green right to life, and you will witness Mother Nature triumphing over the power of man. However, we can certainly end our *own* existence on the planet. Worse than our extinction, in my opinion, would be to live in a land like that of *The Matrix* where we experience the bleakness and lifelessness—consequent of our own maligning actions—or somnambulist inaction.

While the world powers debate global warming, the explosion of population, the hole in the ozone, underwater nuclear testing, the pollution of our waters, the denaturing of our soils, the razing of our rainforests, the spilling of oil into our oceans, the extinction of our animals and insects, we remain on a collision course for a dark future indeed.

Continued debate is no more than a distraction from our reality. Just like the Cold War finally shone a light on the reality that global atomic war means nobody wins, today's G8, G20 or G1 million is the ridiculous spectacle of "rich" countries bullying "poor" countries whereas the reality is, when a power country throws the well-being of a "lesser" country over the cliff, there is a sturdy rope tied to everyone's leg! The balance of Nature from ants to bees to babies and bullies is interdependent, and to think we can pull one of the blocks out as unnecessary, is folly of a most severe consequence.

Who is responsible? Who's at fault? What is to be done? The questions are as redundant and meaningless as, "Will the world end in 2012?" It does not matter.

What matters is that, like that little plant finding its way through the sidewalk each of us must act as if our life depended on it. Because it does.

There is no "them." We can throw bricks at Big Pharma and the addiction of a civilization to pills, and Big Farm and genetically modified grains, to Big Corps for paving the land for theme park condos, or to Big Banks and the avarice of a few that leave the majority in need of food, or jobs, or simple security and peace. But it is you and I and how we continue to buy into the illusion that suggests we need something more powerful than the earth to take care of us.

It is our own consumerism that drives and feeds these giants and bullies. We think they are too big to battle. But like the little shoot with budding leaves, we can take action for a better world. How? By taking responsibility for our every action. Corporations are in power because we pay them to be. Clean air, pure water, and wholesome foods are at a premium because we have settled for less. We have the ultimate power over all these megaliths because we are consumers. And without our dollars they do not thrive.

Now, I'm not bashing wealth creation and the necessity of global organizations to manage the needs of our growing population, but not at the cost of human freedom, or a devastated planet. Better yet, with our consciously directed dollars they continue to thrive by serving our broadest needs.

Proof of this is can be found in your local grocery store. Organic meats, fruits, and vegetables are available where they were not a handful of years ago. We still pay more, but as we demand by our spending habits, those premiums will diminish. This will force agriculturalists to restore the land to be life sustaining. There will be profit in it and that will mean farmers can make a living from providing wholesome food.

And while we're at it, let's look at the balance of Nature in our own bodies. We are a system of interactive and cooperative activity that keeps our cells replicating and our heart beating. How mindful are we of the delicacy of our own bodies? Do we care for them well, or do we stress our bodies, minds, and spirits to the max and then look for an antidote?

Do we live in fear and expect anything other than a fearful outcome? Are we willing slaves to a mortgage, a job, a marriage that undermines our sense of self-worth? As conscious beings capable of choosing our thoughts and actions, we are the very microcosm of what the world herself reflects back to us. There are things we can't do and things we can do. When news of the world's crises real and imagined seem to be overwhelming and out of control, be mindful of what you might do in this moment.

Can you hold back a tsunami? Can you stop the world banks from collapsing? Can you accept that some cataclysms of Nature are inevitable shifts and some cataclysms of man's folly are also inevitable because they are unsustainable—holistically? What might you do? Get busy with the small things in your control and you will find that the images of world cataclysm will fade as you feed a child who is hungry, save the habitat of an endangered animal or insect, plant a tree, buy local food, eat whole foods that have been raised with consciousness or just sit quietly with a good friend.

Every day of your life you are blessed with air and water, food for your belly, and food for your soul. No matter where you live, in the midst of a concrete urbanscape, a desert, meadow or village, you can look up to see the vastness of the sky and the blue of infinite and limitless possibility.

As a child of the earth, you are also a blessing to all living beings. Your smile is as warming as a ray of sunlight, your touch as gentle as a breeze, your kind word as nourishing as food, your tolerance of another's right to be different a breath of fresh air, and your reverence for Life itself the very font of Love that sustains us all.

In closing I'll leave you with these words by Margaret Mead: "Never believe that a few caring people can't change the world. For indeed that's all who ever have."

Love Is All There Is
3 of 3

The ironic truth about 12:21:12 or other predictions of doom.

Wouldn't it be funny if the Mayan Calendar just ended because the stone wasn't big enough? Actually on my theme of it doesn't matter—this is included. But wait! Here is the irony of the age we find ourselves in: While nothing matters, everything counts. *Whaaaat?* Let me explain...

There is a quickening of time—there is no doubt about that. We seem to be hurtling forward into our future and in these weeks before Christmas it is double and treble pace as we try to fit in holiday plans, shopping, and parties into the already overwhelming to-do list.

And while you continue to skip along your personal yellow brick timeline of self-fulfillment and discovery, Earth is spinning mid-latitude (halfway between the equator and the poles) at about 800 miles per hour, day in, day out. Whew! We're moving!

Now, between the relative eternity of the earth's life—a few billion years hence in relation to ours, duration unknown—there is a vast and infinite pool of potential and possibility for every living person. And here is where "nothing matters" but "everything counts" creates the alchemy of a rich life, well loved. (I made a typo and decided it read better than my intended "well lived.")

There are things in this life over which you have no control whatsoever. The spinning Earth, for example. There are things in life over which you have some control. The garbage piling up in landfill sites, for example. And then there is the arena of play where only you are in charge. Your own life!

"But...but...but," you say. "My job, my kids, my mortgage...I'm not free to choose—I don't even have time to choose!"

Take a 360° look at your day—right now. Who is in it and what's going on? These are the parameters of your present playground. These are the constructs—including circumstances and relationships that you have created by your thoughts and actions. Today is a manifestation of all thoughts leading up to this moment.

Now take another 360° turn and look at the world you live in. Every manifestation by man—including the way nails are driven into drywall and the way wars are fought (or that they are fought at all), the way we feed ourselves and don't make sure others are fed; the way we shop, pay for goods, download music are all—*all*—thoughts manifested. Everything. *Everything* began with a thought in one mind and was shared until it became an action of creation and then it became a condition—the nail, the war, the Internet.

Our consciousness as humanity is visible on Earth. The consciousness of All Creation (God by whatever name) is visible as Earth and the cosmos. We have the freedom and the free will to impose our consciousness on the pristine backdrop of this green and blue globe—one thought at a time.

Now if you think that is a stretch, think on this. Consider Google. Google surpassed any other search engine contenders for the simple reason that it delivered higher quality links faster and gained customer satisfaction and then customer loyalty. We want what we want when we want it and Google delivers it best...at the moment. Now Google is not a group of gremlins who read every word printed on a website, nor do they personally assess what range of interests you or I search for. So ask yourself this: How do I only get Google ads for things that I might be interested in?

Google is an algorithm—a mathematical construct. Its "consciousness" is mechanical. It does not judge between bombs and babies. It gives you what you ask for when you ask for it. Last year the count of websites was 182 million and it is doubling as I write. Every day there are hundreds of millions of searches on Google alone. What is the significance of that? Only that at the beginning of every search from every corner of the world is a pair of fingertips tapping on keys. Google responds objectively to every human inquiry regardless of gender, race, religion, status or fame.

Facebook shows us, at a glance, where people's thoughts are, what interests them and what their predominant outlook is. Happy? Conflicted? Self-consumed or Self-actuating? There it all is with photos and video links.

Now, I'm not saying Google is God. Absolutely not! Google has a team of programmers for the algorithm continually tweaking the equation to catch those who would abuse the system and to filter out nefarious content—or at least warn users. God/Life/Creation doesn't do that. Free will is just that. We are each on our own recognizance. We will answer for our choices sooner or later—and that future seems to be rushing to greet us.

Who will we answer to? Is God going to punish us? Will we go to hell? No and no. I think we answer to ourselves and that is punishing enough. If we could only grasp it, we would know our culpability in the state of this world and alter it right now. There is no them. There is only you and I!

What were you doing right before you started reading this? Do you have a backlog of work and a demanding boss? Do you have a "forelog" of household and holiday stuff that must get done? Are you stressed by finances, the state of your significant relationships, the loss of your personal time, your space? Are your dreams a fast-fading mirage on the distant horizon of some tomorrow?

Change it. Change it right now. Nature will show you. Depending on your stomach and intensity of desire you might choose a cataclysm—I like a mountain-toppling earthquake—or the gentle erosion of wind and water until you have a grand and beautiful landscape.

Before you choose, be aware of this: Creation, by its very nature is run on mathematical equations—sacred geometry—the Golden Mean. We see it in the swirl on the shell, the ratio of our body dimensions, and in the Milky Way. The energy that drives that equation is the power of Pure Love. Unconditional Love. The Love of Creation for Herself—in all Her parts—you and me included. Love is the driving force of all Life and the expansion of our experience and the evolution of our universe.

When we stem the flow of nature, we get a lot of stress. When we choose to let Nature flow where She will, we get a lot of energy and a rush to fulfillment. Love loves Life and Life loves Love. Once you remove the sticks clogging the river of your own passion for Life, Life itself will lift you up and into the flow of abundance and joy!

Some people will stay in your life and some people will go. Just know that when you free yourself, you free those whose lives you touch with their own freedom to choose. Your relationships—personal, business and social—will never be the same. They will be better or be gone. If they go, know that they go to have other experiences that will bring them to the knowing of their Self as Life intended it. Each of us, remember, is on our own personal timeline and our experience on Earth not only affects us, but those around us and then, by our collective choices and consciousness, the world itself.

And if you think you fear change, then think on this. Every thought you have will find its sister or brother in others' thoughts until there is a river of thought that will act of its own volition to create some circumstance or relationship. This in turn creates an expanding experience into the world. When you put your fingers on your computer keyboard or phone or whatever gizmo connects you to the digital consciousness of the Internet, what are you asking to come into your life? Now, what thoughts are you asking the Universe, infinitely more objective, but Loving and expansive power to bring into your life?

When you truly understand the power of Love, all fear will dissolve. The prospect of 2012 will dissolve into the pure potential of today. And when you live every day to its fullness of love and gratitude for the beauty of this world, even death will hold no fear.

The Shattering

Breaking through the glass ceiling of ascension.

It seemed like slow motion once the bowl's edge slipped off the upper shelf. Silent descent until it hit the counter with an explosion. Glass flew everywhere, across the kitchen, scattering over the floor, peppering my skin and finally thousands of sparkling beads lay still, crusting the countertop, and resting quietly in leftover dinner.

It was a mess on such a scale and at such an hour that the temptation—*the very great temptation*—was to close the door and deal with it in the morning. With a sigh and a mutter, I faced the inevitable. First off, tomorrow's dinner was wasted. Next I started from an outer radius, gingerly sweeping everything into a glittering heap. It wasn't until my final sweep over the counter with a damp cloth that a tiny shard unzipped the skin on the inside of my thumb.

I let out a series of tiny bleats as the blood gushed and the cool running water seared the cut—excruciating even in its tininess. Athan came running—wakened by my yelps—to find me hand over head, challenging blood against gravity, thumb wrapped in bloodied paper towel and the beginning of tears of pain and…bewilderment.

I don't know why I thought self-actualization would be like Scotty beaming me up into the ethers of divine bliss. I guess I was of the impression that in spirit everything happens effortlessly. And my experience is that, when in spirit—inspired—synchronicity *is* enacted and wondrous events *do* collide. The more we trust the evidence the more it happens. The sticky point is this, though:

Living an inspired life—fired by your own individual spark of the brilliant flame of all that has ever been created and all that may ever be created—is to live *in,* as well as *beyond,* the boundaries of our world as we know it.

Our world as we know it is the microcosm of family and relationships that spirals out to include our vocation, service, goals, aspirations, and into our contribution to the evolution of our community, nation, and globe. Some of these constructs limit us and some of them liberate us. But as long as we are in a limit vs. liberate state of mind, we will be beneath the glass ceiling, gazing at a benign blue sky with white clouds sailing in dreamy, filigreed wisps. It will be in our range of vision but not within our grasp. I am reminded of the most sure and humane way to catch a wild monkey, which is to put nuts in a narrow mouthed jar. The monkey will not let go of its prize even while his fist keeps him prisoner of the jar. Just letting go would free him, but that is never an option.

And what does that have to do with ascension?

And what is so *desirable* about ascension anyway?

Well, it wasn't until the next morning just before 7:00AM that the dawning came. It came with the screech of metal scraping metal, and the echoing crash of blocks of concrete dropping from a great height into a bin. And behind all this jarring cacophony was the insistent and repetitive clatter of a pneumatic drill. No Orcish mine could sound more malevolent to the ear and psyche. This has been going on for three months or more.

My thumb was still throbbing within two Band-Aids as I cracked open the white wooden shutters and gazed into the gaping edifice of the construction site across the road. I could sail a paper airplane onto the upper deck that was now bare concrete. Beneath it laid a vast open space, defined by bare, rusty-looking COR-TEN girders. Rubble the size of footballs was being shoved into noisy piles by a dusty Cat and buckets full of concrete dropped from a great height into the open maw of the dumpster. "More concrete blocks!" was the silent shout to the teams that were grappling with the drills. Even as I write this, the very apartment shakes with this reckoning of what was once constructed.

You see, the building that once housed a theatre, home to Toronto International Film Festival (TIFF), and all kinds of special films is morphing into what rumor has as another place for coffee in our trendy little community of trendy little cafés. The significance to this essay is not what is was or is going to be, but that it is not a demolition and rebuild; it is a deconstruction and redesign. "Aha!" said I to the universe, in sudden awareness of the clear message and the reason for the cut thumb and my own bewilderment.

It goes like this. Stacked in my foyer are bundles of new packing boxes, rolls of bubble wrap, and a basket full of tape and nifty tape dispensers. In three weeks this lovely apartment, my home for two-and-a-half years, will be empty. My stuff? In a vast, dark, and disorderly storage unit that has the stuff of the move from my home before that. Where am I going? Well, first to California to be with my sons for Christmas in less than a month. What was that? My sons are in California? Didn't I mention that?

Oh, well there's the thumb thing. The night of the shattered glass was my younger son's twenty-third birthday. We toasted via Skype. It was the first significant date apart. Together with his older brother, he is euphorically following his star on the west coast. They are in the right place. I know that. I am happy. In my heart, I knew that, like an animal mother, I needed to hold a space until they were ready to hunt in the wild for themselves. Now they are ready, and now they are gone. But my innate knowledge doesn't mean that these separations and transitions are without their cuts and bruises. It is a severing of ties and a reordering of the blocks of love so that there is a bridge, not a fortress.

Ironically, when we first moved into the apartment, our new digs after selling my home in the country, Athan called me over to the window. "There you see, the universe has a message for you!" My sons had found an apartment in the edgy part of town and were tentatively probing the musical dark of the city; it was the first stretching of the umbilical. Following Athan's gesture, I looked across the road. And there, the enormous billboard on the theatre blasted the coming attraction: *The Kids Are All Right*.

But that is only part of the deconstruction. After California, we are making a stop back in Toronto to pick up essentials for the next six months in Greece and Italy. If that sounds cool…it is. But there is more to it than a gadabout. We are leaving here and going there with no firm destination. We've talked about moving to Italy where the weather is more benign, the reverence for age is more profound, and fruit, vegetables, and clear-running springs are abundant. We have created online businesses that Wi-Fi will permit us to run from anywhere. We don't know if we'll like it, but we'll certainly find out!

And if we don't; what then? We don't live here anymore. There is no back to come to.

We are in the process of deconstructing our life here and are in that vulnerable state of no new shell. It is an extremely odd feeling. Not unpleasant. Rather exhilarating. I have been defined by "place" all my life. Now my actions and inactions, my pondering and desires will define me.

Over the past months, since the transition began, I find myself a stranger in my own clothes. I have mysteriously misplaced a box with all my "favorite things." I have given heaps away. I sold a whole set of china that I loved and have collected for decades. Gone. No decision of which beautiful mug I will use in the morning. The brown one that I inherited from my sons' apartment will do.

Our next homes will be someone else's for a week or a month. Here and there. Like the crab of repute, we will grab a shell that fits our moment. We will make these places our own by breaking bread, making love, laughing out loud at our fears, and wondering what took us so long to get free.

When we stop off again in Toronto, what will be the essentials that I pick up to start our new chapter? By necessity I have to travel light, but I still seek to make a nest. What tiny paintings, favorite books, mementos will quickly comfort my little shell-less soul? I have come to know—with a shattering crash and a cut that bled and stung—that ascension or self-actualization is allowing the props to fall away and being okay (even if wobbly and hurting or bewildered) until the transition is integrated.

The soul is our construct—our underpinning of nature and desires and talents and love. The more clear we become in that, the more magnetic we are to the essentials that truly nurture us and bring us joy—in our work, our relationships, our homes, and in our universe. Letting go of things I love to new homes where they will be cherished is difficult, but has inexorably cleansed me of desires for desires' sake. I only desire what is essential for my happiness and what can travel with me. No longer do I want to accumulate stuff.

I no longer want to accumulate stuff in my head or heart either. And this is the short answer to what is so desirable about ascension or self-realization. Traveling light in the heart makes everything that is beautiful your own. I don't have to *have* it for it to please me and infuse me with delight. I no longer have to feel that I don't measure up to anyone's standard or value structure. I am stripped, my little self shattered, and in letting go, I can truly soar.

I have no doubt that the altitude will take some breathing practice and for a while I think I won't look down. As I sort and pack what I need now, next month, what I will need in six months and perhaps what might be shipped when we find a landing point of our own, this mantra I will borrow from Julian of Norwich: "All shall be well, and all shall be well, and all manner of things shall be well."

Why all this convoluted theory about breaking glass and bulldozers? It is this: We don't understand the value of our process unless we *know* we are in active progress. And it is only while we deny it, that we cuss our clumsiness or the vagaries of progress, that we live in a cold, unyielding world. When you are watching it, the universe absolutely speaks on every breath of wind or crash of concrete. Nature is not only the organic and ephemeral, but also the material world that we as natural human beings have seen fit by whatever logic or sensibility to create. When we understand through our clearing of our personal debris, these messages really hit home and offer a GPS tracking signal to our highest purpose. Not necessarily to the final destination but certainly to the most illustrative route imaginable—and oftentimes far beyond our imagination.

I Looked Down and I Got Scared

Getting the hang of gliding.

In *The Shattering* I wrote that once we shatter the glass ceiling of unexamined personal patterns that keep us within view of awakening but out of reach, we could really take flight toward our own fulfillment. In doing just that, I acknowledged that I would need to adjust to this new altitude and promised myself not to look down.

Well, I looked down and I got scared. I watched the ground race up to meet me and imagined plunging deep into the ground as the calico of the checkered countryside in aerial view gave way to dark earth. What happened was I launched myself—kicked off the supports of permanent address, a wardrobe, and my own bed. I found myself traveling with a suitcase of clothes not quite suited to the weather I ultimately experienced. It was off-centering.

Not only that, but I discovered yet again that once your soul gets hold of a willing participant, it travels at lightening speed toward your expressed goal of enlightenment. Enlightenment is not an attained state. It is a recovered state from our inception here on Earth. In plain terms, it is the letting go of all that covers that pure state. That means stuff—material, emotional and spiritual. We can take conscious steps toward it like I did by packing up and living out of a suitcase for a while, but here's the rub: Your subconscious will now take hold of it as well.

Enter disturbing dreams, memories, conflicts, and challenges. Once you've started breaking things up, the iceberg emerges from its depths and great chunks of hard and glittering concepts break off and drop into the frigid soup of denial. I know this happens. I've read about it and I have experienced it when I've done intensive clearing work in the past. And of course here it came again but for some reason, this time I wasn't expecting it. I thought I would have the rewarding experiences of being a risk-taker and a pioneer for my own soul. Out comes the sun and *tra-la-la*—off I go into my new life.

But I got caught in a snare of circumstance. A little one. And the more I tried to shake free, the more entangled I got. I tried to gently disentangle, keep my eyes averted, but the slightly sinister smile of a known pattern was beckoning me closer and showing me that, to get free, I was going to have to do some cutting. I was going to have to look closely at this and see it for what it was—a chance to be free once and for all, or a slide into the recycle bin to come up yet again.

Patterns emerge with new people and slightly different scripts, but the essence remains. Asking you to be more aware of where you place your energy. My patterns are different from your patterns and the details are interchangeable. The problem is when we look but do not see. We get caught in the drama, lights, action, and costume, and overlook the production notes. What is the underlying theme of this scene? What will the drama bring to light, center stage? In my case the play unfolded yesterday—New Year's Day—after a super celebration with my love and my two sons high in the Hollywood Hills, overlooking this city of hope and promise. At midnight, fireworks played across the cityscape and along to the faraway shore of the Pacific recognizable in the distance by its dark expanse and absence of light. We toasted to a glorious 2013.

By evening, a series of individually innocuous events conspired to drive me to a dark memory, seemingly unbidden. It was the retelling of my brother's suicide. As I told the story to my love, he listened patiently while I alternately held back tears and let them flow. One suicide story led to another. First my aunt's, when I was nine, then my grandfather's when my mom was fourteen, and finally my own meager play in my early twenties. Why were these events inserting themselves into my sunny California chapter?

Well, it's like this. I know that I am in the midst of a major shift. Oddly, it seems the whole world is too. I guess we are all doing it together. As I told the stories, which Athan had heard before, we became aware of the synchronistic context. What became evident were the many recent returns to dates and places that were impacted by these events. Events that reached back before I was born. Behavior patterns that find a solution through suicide are mighty powerful. And no matter what your take on the act, the fallout is as resonant through a family as nuclear fission.

So on the eve of the first day of 2013, I found myself falling fast to earth. I had come to California on the first leg of an epic adventure and I was in a rented apartment with broken tiles and a leaking roof. It was freezing. "How", I asked myself, "did I get here?" I went with the meltdown and like a petulant child, wailed that I wanted my beautiful sofa, my own bed, and that I wanted to go *home*. It was not lost on me that, as I directed both space heaters toward the bed and arranged my coat over me and thrust my head into the pillow, that I had no home.

The next morning I woke with an emotional hangover and lay there inventorying my reality checklist. The yin and yang of leaky roofs and cold rooms was that we were tucked into a magical corner of the Hollywood Hills, which has such an energy that can only be experienced. The espresso pot was steaming up rich scents as Athan called a cheery, "Good morning, sunshine!" when he heard me stirring. I was a bit slow shaking off my mood, but we took ourselves out into the canyon and let the trails winding up through the hills toward the HOLLYWOOD sign work their magic.

The trails are broad and meander through shade and sun. Lots of people jog or walk in leisure, accompanied by dogs and horses. There are birds singing and the rustling in the canyon as it drops away might be a coyote—many of whom show themselves without due concern. It is quiet and still but for the breezes. In the distance, Los Angeles stretches out and ends at the Pacific. It's a bit breathy for the first ascent and then the body finds its stride.

The peace between Athan and me was like holding hands. Up and up we went, marveling at the rugged wilderness that fell away at our feet. In a couple of hours we reached the topmost point beneath the mighty white sign. Being now adventurous, we picked our way out onto a promontory to get a backward glancing photo of the sign that would take in its entire famous sprawling letters.

As we walked the jabber of our minds quieted, which was inevitable, it seems, steeped in such tranquil beauty. I began to parse together the bits of experience and make some sense of this juncture. What I realized was that we can stay aloft and maintain a broader perspective, or we can fall into the earthbound dramas that hold us wrapped, for the most part in fear. I had chosen to pick through the bones of the dramas rather than see the pattern of their message.

Once I shifted, this is what I discovered: Like a kite, our flight for freedom is subject to up drafts and down drafts and the quirkiness of the physical world. As we drop patterns and baggage and use memories and lessons as guideposts, we get the up drafts. In time, our wings unfold and we are lifted and learn to maneuver in the higher altitudes. I had made a leap into the air and counted on my wings doing the rest, not heeding that my feet were still entangled on the ground by the certain unconscious dramas. The doldrums passed in the new days of the year spent with Athan and my sons exploring the coast, visiting seals, and peeking in on San Francisco. Unknown to me then, the final release from the tether that bound me was awaiting some weeks later, in the desert far from the sea and the lights.

Hollywood Hooray!

What beats at the heart of Hollywood?

The idea of swinging cats doesn't appeal to me, so let's swing a cheap replica Oscar statuette—anywhere in Hollywood—and you are bound to graze someone in the music or film business. This is the town of entertainers and entertainment—from one end of the spectrum to the other and everything in between.

You will see familiar faces at the grocery store or sitting at the next table in the café, and then the game begins: "Oh, that's...you know... remember that movie?" Snippets of conversations as fellow hikers on the Hollywood Hills trails pass by, including words and phrases like, "scripts," "angel investor," "so I said to my agent..."

On any given day, you will see a young twenty-something kid with printed directions in hand stop with a reverent here-at-last gaze at the surrounding buildings and then trudge on with bulging suitcase in tow. They are arriving. In other places, the paparazzi cluster, barely disguising their telephoto lenses behind hats. Their heads jerk this way and that as their keen eyes follow movement like birds of prey. That's how you know "someone" is nearby. The day before Christmas, Nicki Minaj was busy doing a last-minute jaunt and last week we heard that Brad Pitt was out walking in L.A., with the children in tow. We missed him, but are certain we recently shopped at a small boutique alongside Megan Fox or someone who looked just like her.

The actor who owned the first house we stayed in was recognizable from films and sitcoms, but you might not know his name. The first time we met, he was sweeping out his garage wearing jeans and a pajama shirt. The owner of the second house we stayed in was a producer of known films and headed out to Sundance Film Festival the day before we left. My sons moved into an apartment and discovered the guy across the hall was a music producer. Imagine their delight when he allowed them to play a guitar given to him by none other than the great Johnny Cash.

One day we picked up a little book called *The Gift* at the juice bar in Franklin Village. It was a self-proclaimed synthesis of the various motivational books of our time, but it was told in few words within the relevance of the author's own experience. We went back the next day to pick up another, only to find the little stack all gone. On asking we were told that the author was in most days and if I left my card, they would have him call. Well he called, and when we walked into the shop, there was another familiar face – David Dayan Fisher – one of the bad guys from *National Treasure*.

David shared with us that he started acting late – at twenty-eight. Against all the naysayers he came to Hollywood from England and 'made it'. Every soul is called to its art. Whether we heed it or not is another matter. If we do follow the call of our soul, then we embark on the path of the epic life. Life lived large – not necessarily on the billboards and in the ratings, but in the expansion of our own experience.

When we follow our art we inevitably come face to face with our own doubts and limitations. It is in facing these down that we ultimately 'make it', whether we get another part or not. David realized that he wanted to live life on his own terms. He acts, paints and writes. The proceeds from his books are donated to caring for stray animals in Hollywood. He works out, hikes the hills with his dogs, does yoga, meditates and eats for vitality. He knows that true freedom comes from within and he lives that truth. His book, *The Gift*, shares that story.

I tell you this not for the luster of it, but to facilitate the underlying thrum of this place called Hollywood. Its heart beats on creativity and the striving for personal expression. Now, there is the "star maker machinery," to quote Joni Mitchell, that gathers up the handful of marketable faces as commodities, and there is the entertainment business that gives and takes millions of dollars to dictate tastes and then panders to them, churning out films and music of questionable artistic quality.

Attaining the golden heights of stardom is as within reach for most folks as are the marble-sized diamond stud earrings in the shop on Rodeo Drive. And those heights are not always desirable. They must be precarious to cling to. Can they still retain the freshness of innovation and creativity, not to mention self-mastery? There is often a trade-off in there.

While that stratosphere represents the lion's share of the money, and the big bucks inevitably circulate within few hands, the rest of the population of artist/performers are busy following their hearts and fulfilling their artistic longing. Many have other jobs between gigs because, for most, this industry is not about steady work. But it is this very willingness to live on the edge of uncertainty for the sake of realizing a dream that is what this town is really about. You can feel it.

To paraphrase my son, if the continent of North America was tipped on its edge, you would see talent of all kinds flow to that little district of Hollywood in the big city of L.A. that rests between the Pacific Ocean and the foothills of the San Gabriel Mountains. It is the threshing floor that polishes the brightest and spits out those who lack the searing conviction that this is the life for them. Making it isn't necessarily about being a star. Making it for an artist is about doing what you love to do and getting paid for it. It's also about living within a culture of others doing the same thing. A place where being an artist is a respected profession. And this is that place.

There is a friendliness and openness to newcomers, because this is essentially a place populated by strangers. Coming from the Northern sensibilities of insular living and constant striving for material success often at the expense of our creative selves, this atmosphere is like oxygen. There is a vibe here. No doubt about it.

In his new book, *The Icarus Deception*, Seth Godin calls us all to find our personal art and express it on canvas or within the chapters of our lives. Stepping out of the confines of our structured lives and onto the stage of our own fulfillment asks for a belief in ourselves that many of us haven't yet developed fully.

Hollywood is the context where you can believe in the art of being "you." There is this whole marvelous arena of life beneath the stars that is rich with diversity and beauty and originality. In the ethers of stardom, the machine is not fueled by originality but by sameness. Who will be the "new" Angelina Jolie or Brad Pitt rather than who will be the new and inspiring original? Imagine having to sing outside your key for the rest of your life, rather than belting out your own anthem.

There are many Hollywoods peopled by beggars and stars. The Hollywood I love is the one that welcomes me as I am and inspires me to express that out loud. The Hollywood atmosphere for us was like plasma. Not the flashy streets so much as the hills and the people. Hills very like the low mountains that surround Athens with sweet scented herbs of thyme and rosemary. We found we couldn't leave and so for another two months let the magic of this place and its curious reminder of Greece become a natural segue.

Morning in Athens

Waking up someplace else.

Often awake before dawn, I hear the first bird send out a tentative chirp or two. Unanswered, he is quiet again for sometimes as long as half an hour before the rest of the gang catch on that a new day has, indeed, begun. Singing begins in earnest from the community that nests in the rippled terracotta roof tiles of the Greek Regency style house across the way, here on Filappapos Hill.

I drift in and out of sleep until my thoughts, like the birdsong, tentative at first, begin to tumble over themselves and a story or an observation demands to be written down. I love these mornings. They are days when I am most alive because the earth moves through me in song and sound and sensation. I must write like I must breathe.

Here in Athens, the modern is tentative but the ancient prevails. Orientation is always in context of the Acropolis which, high on its hill, dominates the city. Day or night, sunlight, moonlight or nightlights, the Parthenon stands still, yet pulses with a message thousands of years old. It is the call of integration. A light of awareness that we seem to have all but snuffed out in our drive for achievement and "betterment" rather than personal excellence. We have become specialized, fractioned, disassociated. We are disassociated within ourselves, our minds whipping our trusty bodies like steeds to keep up. This is a place where warriors were trained to peak condition by the play of games. Now, as human beings we are disassociated from our own natural home and our place in it.

I realize here, where I don't speak the language and the alphabet is such that I can't yet make out the simplest of signs unless there is an English translation, that I have lived most of my life on autopilot. This is dramatically different from living in the flow. In the past, I have charted a course and then run it till its completion. Distractions unsought were an annoyance and soon dispatched and distractions sought out—like Facebook—mind-numbing sinkholes for boredom.

Here, modern living—like cars and higher density apartment buildings—has to manage its integration around the ancient that will not be moved. Streets meander and small, efficient cars or sometimes, puffing little hybrids of truck and motorcycle park in a jumble wherever space can be negotiated between overflowing garbage and recycling bins. Steps run up and steps run down and it seems like in a song lyric from *Fiddler on the Roof*: "And one more leading nowhere, just for show." Dogs wander free and there is no evident sensitivity to ownership, bathing, neutering or leashing dogs, let alone scooping. All of this means that, while out walking, you watch your step. Cobblestones may be intact or maybe not. The ubiquitous yellow taxis are legion and navigate these curving streets with amazing speed and dexterity. Tour buses sail around serpentine corners like cartoons seeming to bend in the middle, tilting on the turns and barely missing parked cars by millimeters.

What this does is put you very much "in the now." No talking on your cell as you walk the streets. You need to hear the cars racing up behind you so you can hop into the slip of a space between those that are parked. These are streets pre-automobile, so they are narrow and often one way. Pedestrians beware! After the culture shock realization that not all societies care if things are as modern and efficient and glamorous as possible, you begin to relax. You let peeling wooden shutters, crumbling walls, and surprising bits of ancient floor tiles defying the overtaking grass begin to inform you of a different way of living.

Athens and all of Greece is under economic siege right now. But it seems that through this duress, her riches are being revealed in unexpected ways. Athan and I have come here for this. We have left our world of good, better, best. Of glass condos spiking every vantage point with the glittering reflection of themselves. Of cars and dogs and finely dressed children worn like accessories. We are here for the renaissance.

And what renaissance is that? Just this. The call from the Acropolis for all men and women to listen to their hearts, speak their minds, adore their bodies, revere nature and search for the very heights of all that they as human beings can achieve. Waking every day to the Parthenon offers a life-changing perspective of what man might be and what man actually is.

A few days ago, the streets of Athens shut down and army, police, and special forces tacked out with Flex vests and shin guards, shields and holstered guns, clustered and directed pedestrian traffic. Blockades of police buses parked end to end like a locomotive wound around park and monument, until only a small aperture allowed people to spill along the inside edges and view the parade. It was the commemoration of the liberation from the four-hundred-year siege of the Ottoman Empire two hundred years ago. A small group of protestors shouting about the latest Cyprian banking travesty were closely watched while the song of freedom blasted out from a loud speaker. "Freedom or Death!" was the battle cry that won over the Turkish occupation. It is this statement in nine syllables that is symbolized by the nine blue stripes of the Greek flag.

Freedom. We take it for granted and maybe don't guard against its dissipation while we are distracted with triviality. I read once that as freedoms are quietly usurped, they are replaced with license to act out, which is the evil twin of freedom. Just like the police "allowing" the protestors to rail against the European Community and the arbitrary usurping of their bank accounts distracts the populace from the real menace. And that menace is *fear*. Fear that we have no power and fear that what we have grown up to trust is no longer trustworthy. Fear that our protectors are our violators. Insidious.

As insidious as the rape victim shamed for her complicity in the violation of her entire being.

And standing calmly in the suns and rains of centuries on a high hill overlooking the comedies and tragedies of this day, is the Acropolis, where millions of footfalls over centuries have polished the red porphyry and grey/white marble into smooth and slippery stones. Monuments to freedom from tyranny, freedom of speech, freedom of mind, freedom of love, and freedom to seek out truth.

Greek—or I should say Hellenic—architecture, philosophy, art, language, science, astronomy, and medicine are the underpinnings of the cultivated world, which elsewhere enjoyed the renaissance beginning in the 1400s. History has it that the fall of Constantinople and the beginning of the Ottoman occupation saw many Hellenic scholars leave Greece, taking the ancient books, their gold and ideas to Florence, where they inspired a movement that would spread through all of Europe, but leave their own country sadly in the darkness of tyranny. And then not so long ago the country gained a wobbly freedom only to be subjected to a yoke of another kind. In the tavernas when the bouzouki player sings, every mouth moves with the words, some in silence, some out loud. Songs of the fight for freedom, love lost, heartbreak; the words known by every generation gathered around tables laden with simple traditional foods.

I love this country and can feel the fierce loyalty these solid people have to their mountains, their fields, their trees, their seas, their traditions, and their heritage. For now it is my home, too.

Aegina Island

Sailing on Cerulean Seas

Hellas—the spirit of freedom, excellence, and beauty.

A tiny sailboat bobs on the whitecaps accenting the teal blue waves. I have stopped to watch as it makes its way along the backdrop of the distant island of Salamis. Nearer, gulls catch the currents on this breezy morning and circle in slow spirals above the small harbor where the little fishing boats gather. It is my daily view—always the same, yet always changing. Shortly a huge blue and white ferry with its unmistakable red smoke stack will glide by silently, slicing through the waves with just a froth at its bow.

The ferries are regular and predictable. In all but the most severe winter seas, they will keep to schedule and transport people and cars to and from the islands and the busy port of Piraeus. From the many port gates serving the various island groups—Saronic (where we are), Cycladic, Ionian—ferries let off passengers who whizz off by car, impatiently disgorged from capacious bellies to the nearby highway, or pedestrian travelers, who walk briskly to the metro station where, within minutes, they will be in downtown Athens.

But it is the sailboat I am watching. It is I who am bobbing on a glorious spirit that is Greece—or better-described: Hellas. I have come to this land with my Hellenic life partner and sweet love, Athanasius, thinking we would stop in, see family and take off for an adventure in Italy. Instead, after traversing the mainland from the mountains and seas in the north to the mountains and seas to the south, we are here on the island of Aegina, quite by serendipity.

White curtains billow at the open terrace windows, of our little house overlooking the strait that will be home for the next year. A small chime with Chinese characters dances with a sweet, tinkling tune, until a gust sends it clanging. As the sun has now risen, the sea has turned a deeper blue—almost royal—and the distant freighters at anchor waiting to offload in Piraeus have emerged from the morning mist into more distinct shapes.

Directly across from our little house, on the rise above the sea, is what appears to be a giant sea serpent lumbering just below the surface, with rounded stone back and rump and tail visible as if it were about to arise to its full mightiness. Beyond is Salamis or Salamina—where the famed battle to conquer the Persian invaders succeeded—and behind that, the mountain ranges of the mainland. Each formation is less distinct as they recede into the mists and finally merge with the sky softened blue grey at the punctuated horizon. In the evening purpled light, we have counted six distinct layers, ancient rounded and craggy massiveness, settled on the straight line of the Aegean.

I feel I have pushed off from known shores in my little boat and have caught the gentle wind that fills my sail and sets me skimming across the waters of infinite possibility. The sea is my soul and the boat is my will. I am no longer anchored by expectations—my own or others'—and I am feeling the wind in my hair and the sun on my skin. I have freed my will and aligned it with the will of creation. I am willing to be taken where it is most fulfilling and joyful for me to be. And that place is here.

Hellas or in modern usage, Hellada, is a land of such abundance that to think of it only in images of islands of whitewashed houses with cobalt blue shutters set against ultramarine seas, is to see only the bright ribbon on a very large and lavish gift. This land is so rich and diverse and resplendent, with a spirit of such humility, that it is awe-inspiring. The humility rises from a people whose very DNA remembers The

Athenian Miracle when Greece was greater than any civilization before or since and which seeded the western world with science, art, language, political democracy, the reminders of which still stand on sacred sites in such places as Sounio, Olympia, and Athens. Here on Aegina is the elegant Temple of Ephaia creating a perfect equilateral triangle with the Parthenon on the Acropolis and the Temple of Poseidon at Sounio.

Centuries of wars and occupation which in the north ended less than one hundred years ago; brutal extinction of whole villages and the willful destruction of the ancient monuments, has taken a heavy toll. This is a simple country, mostly rural and in many areas remote; an agricultural land which has been sent racing headlong into a European Community, running as fast as possible, long before it can properly walk on its freedom legs.

While the rest of Europe enjoyed the renaissance inspired by the Greek scholars with ancient texts of Pythagoras, Plato, Hippocrates, and the like, many fled the Ottoman occupation and Greece was submerged by oppression into a land of isolated and distrustful tribes. The Athenian Miracle lasted a brief one hundred years before it lost its own compass, and its leaders—once devoted to the law, freedom, and equality—fell by their own hubris into excess, exploitation, and betrayal.

The irony is that, even today, despite the betrayal by many of its own political leaders and the resulting economic debacle, the country can boast what many cannot; unspoiled tracks of land, crystal waters, thousands of species of plants and herbs. Over one hundred species of olives alone exist when most of the world has become specialized and modified. Vast tracts of wildlife and wildflowers flourish, protected by the isolating and challenging topography of the land. Mountain springs that perpetually flow clean, alive, and pure. And most precious of all, a longevity to be envied by cultures all over the world. Graves show pictures of youthful smiles in ancient weathered faces and the stone is etched with the ages, 102, 90, 98, 114. When someone cited that sixty was the new forty, some octogenarians in the mountains were tending their goats or trimming their vines with a laugh and a song and a sparkle of youth in their eyes.

The wind has risen, though there are fewer white caps now, and the rolling seas are deeper. The water has changed hue to cerulean that to me looks like crushed emeralds and sapphires. My artist friend tells me it is a necessary color added to the pallet of any artist who would paint in Greece. In the bay the harbor embraces the small wooden fishing boats, whitewashed and topped with bright blue canopies that look like they may hail from centuries past. The shallows are aqua and pale celadon green where the waves break over the rocks. There are more sailboats out on the sea this afternoon. I am finding my way in this land of natural beauty, philosophy, and poetry—recalled to a life purpose once abandoned for a "better" idea.

From our Aegina home base, Athan is finding his calling in the land of his birth among the olive groves and other sources of traditional foods, and practices that the ancient Hellenes embraced to assure health and vitality. He is working with researchers to discover the secrets of the Athenian Miracle and the wisdom of Hippocrates: "Let thy food be thy medicine." This he shares in his book, *Recipes for the Revival of the Hellenic Spirit*. And I have embraced the call of the muse and am sharing the rest of my story in *Exhilarated Lifestyle: A Holistic Look at Health and Happiness*.

Together we are developing a line of healing supplements based on wild olives, wild olive leaf, flower essences, and highest quality essential oils—an adventure that will take us to the heart of Italy, Spain, France, and, of course, our own home here in Greece.

Here we are meeting others, many others, who by themselves or in small groups are recapturing the spirit of the land, the culture and its people. It is the spirit of freedom, excellence, and beauty. We are sailing together—separately—kindred to the wind and the ever-changing constant of the soul.

Last winter I ventured into the dark storage locker in Toronto. What few things might I take to our little house to make it home? Our beloved books, yes. A selection of small original paintings to hang on the few walls that are not glorious windows onto the sea. What else? Pieces of china from four families; Treasures that have lived in the back of cabinets or in storage boxes for decades…until now. These include a vintage set of Wedgwood *Ranunculus* which George bought me one Christmas. It was the pattern that my mother had when she married. All that was left of the original set was a small saltcellar that I treasured as a little girl. I love the spray of wildflowers on a creamy white background. Second is a set of four cups and saucers, *Belle Fiore*, which my cousin kindly gave me of her mother's when I told her that the exuberant print always reminded me of my aunt's wonderful laugh. And then there are the two sets of delicate demitasses; one inherited from my father's family, Royal Crown Derby, *Mikado* and the other from my mother's family, Noritake *Fleurgold*. From these we serve Greek mountain tea, olive leaf tea, or espresso. And I have used each with deep awareness and tribute while I was doing this final writing. It is not lost on me that the hands of those I loved and of those long gone before I was born, but whose blood is in my veins, also held these cups and have gently brought them to their lips. They have become daily symbols of integration of all that was love based in my family. I cherish the beauty and release the sorrows. Life has become a simple celebration of every day.

Stringing the Pearls

Holding On to What's Precious

When I got the manuscript for this book back from the editor I was excited to action the changes and send it off to the publisher. But a funny thing happened. I dropped into a reflective funk. My perspective was higher, from a place of calm objectivity, but I experienced a long, slow circling of events and memories that were emotionally charged. What was going on?

I discovered on this self-reflection that I was still identifying on some level with the sad and regretful events of my life. Emotions like fear, anxiety, regret, and anger are remnants of the past that can be reignited when we least expect it. Culturally we are trained to identify with negative emotions and tie experience up with blame or shame. These are the hooks that lodge deeply within us. These are the hooks I experienced as emotional charges as I reviewed the manuscript. Emotions make us react—react without thought. This keeps us stuck.

When I choose to respond with objectivity, I unhook from the emotion. I allow that emotion to exist because the event existed, which, in its moment, created that emotion. The event and its partnered emotion may be recalled as a memory or may be forgotten, but that emotional charge was entered into the data of the cells of our body. It remains waiting to be released.

You can release these emotional charges when you accept that they are part of you (they happened) but they are not YOU. Over the course of the years shared in *Exhilarated Life* and in the intervening time I have discovered strategies to tap in to my inner happiness and innate wisdom, and I now live my soul purpose each day expanding into the next. Where that will lead ultimately is a divine mystery and ongoing adventure. Happiness is a capacity we are born with. It's not a treat for good behavior, as we are trained to believe. Happiness comes in many forms and offers a barometer for assessing experiences and a compass for keeping you aligned with your soul purpose.

Here are the words I use to describe happiness: joy, delight, bliss, fun, enthusiasm, pleasure, creativity, freedom, kindness, appreciation, devotion, gratitude, acceptance, sincerity, synchronicity, inspiration, authenticity, and reverence. When you recognize these in your day, you can see how pervasive happiness really is. Happiness is all around you if you allow it. When listened to, your soul will unerringly guide you to your greatest joy in self-expression. The wisdom of the soul has been ignored for so long that it might take quiet time to coax it out. Once acknowledged, it will bubble forth—wake you in the morning excited with inspiration, enhance your sleep with deep problem solving, and guide you to the perfect people and places in synchronicity. Prepare to be surprised and delighted by your inner wisdom.

Your soul purpose is not an unfathomable mystery to be searched out. It is immanent, fundamental; in every moment you are the total expression of your potential. There comes a sense of completeness and fulfillment with where you are now. This is the most profound lesson I can offer you: Your purpose is not to become, but to be. Be who you are right now. Let moments of happiness guide you to your inner wisdom. Crave to be all you might be and know that each day you are a more splendid, evolved version of your Self. Dream bold sunbursts of dreams. See yourself happy and fulfilled and then hold these images as guiding lights along your path of action. Yes action.

Happiness, wisdom, and purpose don't happen by chance. I have explored my own process, shared it through the stories in *Exhilarated*

Life, and ultimately distilled the lessons into simple yet essential exercises to support you on your path to self-fulfillment. They are necessary and get easier with practice. Make them your daily habits and express your own exhilarated life in happiness, wisdom, and purpose.

Here they are:

Eleven Habits for Happiness

1. **Choice**: This is the privilege of consciousness. It is as immutable as the law of gravity and you ignore it at your peril. But for some reason most of the world and even many of the spiritual and motivational teachers of our time still do not live as if they know it even exists. It is this: What you think and what you take action on will manifest in your life experience. Period.

    What you are experiencing right now is the cumulative effect of every choice you have ever made. You cannot think two thoughts at the same time. Choose what you think about very carefully. You may have some negative thoughts or beliefs but small, frequent, and consistent choices to align to your truth will eliminate any barriers to happiness.

    Change is simple when you understand that and shift your perspective even one degree by taking any small action toward what you desire. Much more subtle than visualization, it is a placement of your focus on the *state* of being you wish to achieve and then allowing the how and the what to present themselves. They will.

2. **Forgiveness**: This is the most difficult gateway, but really the only entrance into the kind of peace and happiness I describe. It is a much-misunderstood practice because in our religious doctrines, we are often taught that forgiveness is an externally directed benevolent acceptance of hurtful acts. It is not.

    Forgiveness is what you grant yourself to be free. It is neither the absolution of others' actions, nor of their responsibility for their actions. Hurtful acts reveal the nature of another person and a willingness to forgive will allow you to see two things. One is that while actions might seem personally directed, they are most often unconscious acts committed by those who are overcome by their own insecurity or lack of self-love. The second, equally valuable insight is that the nature of the injury to you will reveal something in yourself that is not being loved—by you.

When you reflect on events that require forgiveness, you will begin to see there is a pattern. It will be a freeing insight. People and circumstances will fall away from you of their own accord. Let them go.

3. **Love**: This one is simple. Let love be your guide. Surround yourself with people you love. Speak your love. Share your love. Do work that you love and take time to play at what you love. Find a need in the world that speaks to your heart—the pulse of love—and give your love to that.

    Some people are called to build schools in Malawi and some people are called to feed stray cats. Do what *you* love. If you face a challenge or difficulty, bring your loving attention to it. Whether it's a difficult exam or accepting the death of someone dear, magnitude is relative; these are times of deep inner growth and love is the best sun and rain for the most radiant blossoming. If, after forgiveness, someone has to leave your life so that you can flourish unimpeded, let him or her go with love. But first, the greatest gift of love is the one you give yourself. Love yourself *now*.

4. **Being**: Human being, that is. You are spirit, you are flesh and you are consciousness. Separating these elements is like trying to see your reflection in a broken mirror. Thought is what most often breaks this mirror. Align your thoughts through forgiveness and love, and the innate intelligence and collaboration of these aspects of your being will take you to the highest expression of all that you can be.

Your body is your experiencer and informs your mind through all senses—well beyond five. These senses are of your world, the one within, the one without, and the one beyond. Care for your body with nourishing food, clean water, fresh air, movement, and relaxation. Care for your mind with stillness, either through meditation, a walk in nature or some practice that takes you beyond thought and into communication with your deepest consciousness.

To care for yourself is the first act of self-love.

5. **Clarity**: See what you see and feel what you feel and trust that. Keep the state of being you desire—like happiness—clear in your mind and let your feelings and intuition guide you toward that. Be absolutely clear on the fact that human beings lacking developed consciousness can be very destructive. You are bucking the tide.

    Pay attention to what people say and what they do. Do not interpret actions—witness them. If they feel right, trust that. If they do not feel right, respond appropriately to that. Live by your own lights and you shine a light for others to follow. There are no shortcuts to happiness—but there are clear cuts. Create that by being attentive to your inner voice.

    You do not have to explain yourself or give reasons for your decisions. Be completely honest with yourself at all times. Live in the present moment; it is the only time that exists.

6. **Holism**: This is the law of "one." You are sovereign. Everything that you require for the fullest expression of your individuality as a human being is within you right now. It is your purpose in this life to fulfill your own unique potential. You are the power of one. There are no twos or threes or fours. There are only multiples of one. And as nature organizes atoms into molecules and molecules into cells, each stage is comprised of cooperating individuals for the common good of the unit. As human beings

we gather into families and families gather in communities and onward until we have escalating units of multiples of ones up to seven billion, comprising humanity.

Humanity is one unit amongst many collaborating elements that include water, air, land, animals, minerals, and plants, which must cooperate for the highest good of the earth that sustains us all. From here only imagination to the infinite power of one can describe the universe from the atomic to the cosmic. Each element is ultimately necessary.

7. **Breath**: So much more than just taking in oxygen. There is only one. From your first inhale to your last exhale is one continuous breath. It is this precious breath that is your lifeline; your connection to all of life as every being, creature and living entity inhales and exhales.

   In perfect harmony as you exhale, plants and trees inhale, and cleanse the air. As they exhale, you inhale life-giving hydrogen and oxygen in perfect proportion to your physical requirements for optimal health. With every breath you take, every cell in your body is nourished and either revitalized or renewed. As you exhale, expired cells enter into the earth's own breath for recycling. The more deeply we breathe, the more completely our bodies' requirements for rejuvenation are nourished.

   Take time morning and evening or any time during the day, for deep conscious breathing. This is one of the most health-inducing ways to bring peace and calm to your whole being and connect you to all of Life. Draw in the breath slowly and fill your lungs and then empty them completely with a final puff.

   Breathe with conscious attention of how your breath connects you with all of life—from the beginning of time. This will serve to bring you into alignment with your perfect place within the microcosm and macrocosm of our life-sustaining universe.

8. **Simplicity**: KISS—*Keep It Sublimely Simple.* As you release the energies of the past and clear out the basement of your emotional life, take a look at the clutter in your physical life. Not only your material environment of house or workplace, but your social life and the professional commitments you make.

   At the core of your life there are simple needs and a few special objects of meaning. Use these as the basis or foundation for a new simplicity of life. One where you are not overwhelmed to find storage for all that you don't use, or yoked to a job to maintain a lifestyle that is unnecessarily cumbersome financially or in maintenance. We are encouraged on every front to strive for big, better, best, not to give us comfort, but to keep us always in the discomfort of being an underachiever. You have nothing to achieve but your own happiness and peace of mind. Create your palace or sanctuary by honoring yourself with a few special pieces of furniture or art that are precious and meaningful. Size doesn't matter—really—not too small or too large but in terms of management and peace of mind, a size that is just right for you. Keep your social activities and professional commitments limited to those you will really enjoy and participate in fully.

   When you drop unnecessary demands like stones then you will begin to be present to what you do have and find fulfillment in all that is lovely and pleasing.

9. **Mysticism**: Your own intimate relationship with the ineffable. The core principle underlying all religions and spiritual practices is love, no matter how off the rails it has veered through centuries of misinterpretation and misuse. The Divine is not something of static perfection and blind adherence but a personal communication with powers and potentials that we can never really know fully but which actively participate in our evolution. That evolution takes us to heights of fulfillment that have no

limit. There is no limit because, as we achieve higher levels of personal expression of love in all we do, we push the wave of potentiality ever before us, individually and collectively. There is no power that rules us but a field of potentiality that responds to our thoughts and actions. In a way we rule the potentiality. That is why it makes no sense to ask, "If God is love, why does he let terrible things like war and hunger happen?" Annihilating self-interest or love manifest, We drive the outcome collectively. We are all responsible.

What we refer to as Heaven, or Hell for that matter, may well be one magnificent mirror. So, whether it is through artistic expression, chant, music, meditation, prayer or a combination of these and/or other practices, open the communication and trust in the unlimited and divine power of love.

10. **Golden Rule**: This little nugget of a rule is most often broken and would be the one behavior that could change the world. *Treat others as you would have them treat you.* "Others" include: Your family, children, the elderly, strangers, co-workers, employees, employers, people who serve you and people you serve, people you understand and people you do not understand, and people who do not understand you. And it also includes every living thing. We often confuse our relationships in some sort of hierarchy, when there are none greater or lesser than ourselves. Loving kindness is the only currency here and it starts first with you for your Self.

   What we experience in every encounter will shift instantly with a genuine smile, a gentle touch, an act of respect, and an attitude of reverence. You are the conscious one in a world largely unconscious. Beam out your peace and goodwill. You will be delighted at what beams back.

11. **Gratitude**: It is more than being thankful. It is the deepest appreciation for all that is good in our lives and understanding

that 'good' is a relative term that cannot be discerned sometimes until well past the 'bad'. In the meantime, focus on being grateful for the small and large treasures that impress your daily life. Gratitude is a magnet that attracts more and more similar circumstances and experiences into your life. Gratitude is the symbiosis of giving and receiving so that we can be generous in sharing what we have and humble in graceful acceptance of what we receive.

Simple appreciation keeps us in the present moment and imbues our everyday life with the magic of the beauty and abundance that surrounds us always. It is a tuning in with all our senses. Make a habit of noticing these aspects of a fulfilled life. We fly through days without awareness of much other than what crosses our path and demands our attention.

One way to develop this awareness is to focus on our five senses. Take a moment right now and contemplate one sense at a time. Let your eyes open and take in the color of the sky, or the room around you. Draw in a breath and smell the air, fresh with pine or snow or coffee. Taste honey or olive oil or lemon and feel these on your tongue. Hear the sounds of birdsong, traffic or the voice of one you love. Be grateful for your senses and the stories they tell you about the life you are living right this moment. Now, gently run your hands over your face. Feel your skin beneath your fingertips and allow the deepest gratitude for who you are and the life you have right now fill you to overflowing.

Until we meet again, be gentle with yourself and may you find the enduring happiness that is your birthright as a human being on this gorgeous planet.

***

You are a spark
from the brilliant flame
of all that has ever been created and
all that may ever be created.
I am that,
you are that and
that is LOVE.

You are Utterly Unique,
Incredibly Precious,
Unconditionally Loved and
Vitally Necessary.

Télos

Staying Social

Life is a challenge even when you are well armed
with philosophy and strategies.
I welcome you to connect with me through social media
so we can share this adventure together.

Twitter
twitter.com/MarilynHarding

Instagram
instagram.com/marilynharding_writer

Facebook Pages
facebook.com/marilynhardingauthor

Exhilarated Life
facebook.com/ExhilaratedLife

Exhilarated Discussion
facebook.com/groups/652436934859350

Linkedin
linkedin.com/in/marilynharding

Google+
plus.google.com/u/0/+MarilynHarding

Websites
marilynharding.com
exhilaratedlife.com

***

Going Forward

If you enjoyed this book or found it helpful in forging your path to happiness, wisdom and purpose, please leave a review on Goodreads [goodreads.com/book/show/25146416-exhilarted-life] or the site where you purchased it. I will be most grateful for your time and consideration.

***

You may find the companion journal ***Exhilarated Life: 111 Ways to Happiness*** helpful in applying the concepts from this book. Here you will find 111 reflections from the book with recommendations to bring the lessons and achievement of happiness into your daily life. This is a transformational and self-empowering guide and journal where you can discover and record your own intimate and personal journey to fulfillment and self-actualization.

Watch for ***Exhilarated Lifestyle: A Holistic Look at Health and Happiness*** where I share the wisdom of today's masters in nutrition, natural therapies, self-development, personal philosophy and so much more. Coming 2018

Subscribe for news and updates and receive my gift to you, a poster sharing ***Ten Life Altering Truths***. [marilynharding.com/your-free-gift]

***

About the Author

As a marketing executive, entrepreneur, mother and writer, Marilyn Harding has used her bountiful life and career experiences as a spiritual laboratory distilling the complexity of life into the simplicity of inspired living and everyday happiness. Marilyn Harding writes on holistic lifestyle, art, relationships, innovation and travel.

Author of *Exhilarated Life*, a book about gaining clarity and living an *authentic life,* and the illustrated children's book about divorce, "Yesterday At Justin's", Marilyn Harding is a published writer and a frequent contributor on The Huffington Post United States and Greece.

In business, Marilyn Harding is the Director of Artemis Alliance Inc., which fosters strategic alliances in holistic lifestyle research and innovation with a focus on Hellenic (Greek) traditional products and health practices.

Marilyn lives on Aegina Island, Greece with her mate, Athan, basking in love and sunshine, tasting and testing EVOOs and sipping on wine.

***

Notes

www.ingramcontent.com/pod-product-compliance
Lightning Source LLC
LaVergne TN
LVHW041611070426
835507LV00008B/183